# Trump and Autobiography

The 1970s and 1980s heralded the rise of neoliberalism in United States culture, fundamentally reshaping life and work in the United States. Corporate culture increasingly penetrated other aspects of American life through popular press CEO autobiographies and management books that encouraged individuals to understand their lives in corporate terms. Propelled into the public eye by the publication of 1989's *The Art of the Deal*, ostensibly a CEO autobiography, Donald Trump has made a career out of reversing the autobiographical impulse, presenting an image of his life that meets his narrative needs. While many scholars have sought a political precedent for Trump's rise to power, this book argues that Trump's aesthetics and life production uniquely primed him for populist political success through their reliance on the tropes of popular corporate culture. *Trump and Autobiography* contextualizes Trump's autobiographical works as an extension of the popular corporate culture of the 1980s in order to examine how Trump constructs an image of himself that is indebted to the forms, genres, and mechanisms of corporate speech and narrative. Ultimately, this book suggests that Trump's appeal and resilience rest in his ability to signify as though he is a corporation, revealing the degree to which corporate culture has reshaped American society's interpretive processes.

**Nicholas K. Mohlmann** is assistant professor of English at the University of West Florida. He earned his PhD in literary studies from Purdue University.

# Routledge Focus on Literature

**The Rise of the Australian Neurohumanities**
Conversations Between Neurocognitive Research and Australian Literature
*Edited by Jean-François Vernay*

**Neo-Georgian Fiction**
Re-imagining the Eighteenth Century in the Contemporary Historical Novel
*Edited by Jakub Lipski and Joanna Maciulewicz*

**Introduction to Digital Humanities**
Enhancing Scholarship with the Use of Technology
*Kathryn C. Wymer*

**Geomythology**
How Common Stories are Related to Earth Events
*Timothy J. Burbery*

**Re-Reading the Eighteenth-Century Novel**
Studies in Reception
*Jakub Lipski*

**Trump and Autobiography**
Corporate Culture, Political Rhetoric, and Interpretation
*Nicholas K. Mohlmann*

For more information about this series, please visit: https://www.routledge.com/Routledge-Focus-on-Literature/book-series/RFLT

# Trump and Autobiography
Corporate Culture, Political Rhetoric, and Interpretation

Nicholas K. Mohlmann

NEW YORK AND LONDON

First published 2021
by Routledge
605 Third Avenue, New York, NY 10158

and by Routledge
2 Park Square, Milton Park, Abingdon, Oxon, OX14 4RN

*Routledge is an imprint of the Taylor & Francis Group, an informa business*

© 2021 Nicholas K. Mohlmann

The right of Nicholas K. Mohlmann to be identified as author of this work has been asserted by them in accordance with sections 77 and 78 of the Copyright, Designs and Patents Act 1988.

All rights reserved. No part of this book may be reprinted or reproduced or utilised in any form or by any electronic, mechanical, or other means, now known or hereafter invented, including photocopying and recording, or in any information storage or retrieval system, without permission in writing from the publishers.

*Trademark notice*: Product or corporate names may be trademarks or registered trademarks, and are used only for identification and explanation without intent to infringe.

*Library of Congress Cataloging-in-Publication Data*
Names: Mohlmann, Nicholas K., author.
Title: Trump and autobiography : corporate culture, political rhetoric, and interpretation / Nicholas K. Mohlmann.
Description: New York, NY : Routledge, 2021. | Includes bibliographical references and index.
Identifiers: LCCN 2021005628 (print) | LCCN 2021005629 (ebook) | ISBN 9781032025247 (hardback) | ISBN 9781032025278 (paperback) | ISBN 9781003183754 (ebook)
Subjects: LCSH: Trump, Donald, 1946- | Autobiography—Authorship. | Presidents—United States—Biography—History and criticism. | Executives—United States—Biography—History and criticism. | Capitalism—Social aspects—United States. | Neoliberalism—United States.
Classification: LCC E913.3 .M64 2021 (print) | LCC E913.3 (ebook) | DDC 073.933092 [B]—dc23
LC record available at https://lccn.loc.gov/2021005628
LC ebook record available at https://lccn.loc.gov/2021005629

ISBN 13: 978-1-032-02524-7 (hbk)
ISBN 13: 978-1-032-02527-8 (pbk)

Typeset in Times New Roman
by codeMantra

**For April, always**

# Contents

1 Scary Beauty: Towards a Trumpian Aesthetics    1

2 A Genius Purely by Instinct: Simulating Management in *The Art of the Deal*    24

3 A Chevrolet in Tokyo: Lee Iacocca, Japanese Management, and Donald Trump's *Surviving at the Top*    48

4 The President Makes All the Difference: Genre, Image, and Becoming a Business Candidate    76

5 Coda: No More Bullshit: Trump Signs Off    106

*Index*    111

# 1 Scary Beauty
## Towards a Trumpian Aesthetics

As both a candidate for and a holder of the office of president of the United States, Donald Trump generated controversy with what he said as well as how he said it. Some statements were viewed and condemned as offensive, such as his assertion that "when Mexico sends its people, they're not sending their best…they're bringing drugs; they're bringing crime; they're rapists, and some, I assume are good people" or his infamous boast that "when you're a star, they let you do it. You can do anything. Grab them by the pussy. You can do anything" ("Transcript: Donald Trump's Taped Comments About Women"). Other statements were objected to based on their truthfulness, such as Trump's repeated, but unproven, claims that there is substantial voter fraud in the United States.[1] Even when the content of Trump's remarks have been less controversial, his habits of speech have led to speculation about his mental acuity and fitness for office, with some statements, like his discussion of his uncle's work on nuclear technology, reaching a certain meme status for their supposed incoherency (Mikkelson). We might say that Trump's speech has come under fire both for its consistency and for its inconsistency; the ways it consistently marginalizes, prevaricates, and confounds; and how it inconsistently represents reality and breaks with the norms of American political speech in content and form. While one can certainly make convincing arguments that Trump's actions as the head of the executive branch are authoritarian, even destructive, Trump's speech across a range of modalities demands careful attention for the ways he uses it to subvert and manipulate the political and cultural processes that make his executive actions possible.

Unlike other presidential candidates who ran on the strength of their business acumen, like Ross Perot, Trump's success came in part because he has spent much of his life constructing himself as a public figure with certain significations. Through media appearances, book publications, and television programs, Trump produced an image of himself and a narrative of his life that emphasized his extreme wealth and cutthroat business savvy. This image and narrative served a commercial purpose initially, deepening and cementing the connotations associated with Trump's name, a name that became a commodity, marking buildings and products with the Trump brand. In the twenty-first century, Trump leveraged the symbolic capital he had accumulated in the twentieth century by taking to Twitter to push conspiracy theories about President Barack Obama's place of birth and to opine on a wide range of political issues (Krieg). In doing so, Trump added to his brand's signification political and digital dimensions that positioned him to pursue higher office. Thus, when Trump announced his candidacy for president of the United States, he was already familiar and legible to an American audience. A key difference that allowed Trump to disrupt the Republican primary and ultimately assume the office of president is that Trump refused to act "presidential," a sort of contortion of one's public production of one's self to meet an assumed set of norms for a president or presidential candidate's behavior and speech. A common explanation provided for a sizeable voting population embracing a presidential candidate who rejected presidential norms was that voters who backed Trump wanted a disruptive candidate, someone who went against the status quo. In what follows, I would like to suggest that part of Trump's appeal is not simply a rejection of presidential norms that entails an embrace of anything that signifies as anti-presidential, but rather a recognition and acceptance of another set of norms already deeply familiar to nearly all Americans: the forms and mechanisms of commercial corporate speech and identity.

We can see the mechanisms of corporate speech in the struggles Trump's businessperson-as-candidate predecessor Mitt Romney faced in 2012. When Mitt Romney was running for president of the United States, his record as a businessperson received significant attention, positive and negative. As CEO of Bain Capital, a private equity firm, Romney oversaw the acquisition and reorganization of many corporations. As a result, Romney took fire both from Republican primary opponents and from Democrats for decisions that resulted in large layoffs.[2] Romney's image as a slick corporate raider led former presidential candidate Ralph Nader to argue that Romney was, "essentially, a corporation running for president masquerading as an individual" (Nader). Given the 2010 Supreme Court ruling on Citizens United vs. the Federal Election

Commission, a decision that found that corporations count as legal persons whose free speech the first amendment of the Constitution protects, it is not surprising that corporate personhood and the fuzzy line between biological and legal people was on Nader's mind. The press would even skewer Romney for his insistence to an Iowan interlocutor that "corporations are people, my friend" (Oliphant).

Political opponents used this statement to indict Romney along the same lines as Nader, suggesting the claim tied Romney to an embrace of the logic of corporate personhood laid out in Citizens United (Dwyer). However, Romney's response to the protestors is both more nuanced and more illustrative of Romney's actual relationship as a CEO to his firm. Romney's insistence that corporations are people is a response to a protestor calling out that corporations should pay higher taxes. After Romney makes his famous remark, the protestor yells, "No they're not!" to which Romney replies, "Of course they are, everything corporations earn ultimately goes to people." The protestors then jeer as Romney asks, "Where do you think it goes?" to which the protestors yell something like, "In their pockets." As the protestors attempt to shout over Romney, Romney triumphantly declares, "Pockets? Pockets? Whose pockets? People's pockets! Human beings, my friend" (Sargent). Romney's responses, while disingenuous and incomplete, indicate how he conceives of the corporation as a fictional entity. In Romney's thinking, there is a distinction between the fictional person, the corporation, and those who participate in its assemblage, the "human beings," like the workers and CEO who act and speak for and through the corporation. In this instance, Romney manipulates the metonymic relationship between the fictional, non-corporeal corporation and certain components of its assemblage, here people, to separate out one aspect of the corporation and assign that aspect agency. While Romney's embrace of the image and affectations of a CEO lays the ground for Nader's hyperbolic statement that Romney, in essence, is a corporation, Romney generally performed the role of a CEO by negotiating the relationship between CEO and firm in normative ways.

It is surprising, then, that while Romney was accused of being a corporation, Donald Trump, a businessperson who proudly stated in his declaration of candidacy for the presidency, "I'm a private company," has generally avoided the same accusation ("Here's Donald Trump's Presidential Announcement Speech"). As an icon of individualism, scholars have placed Trump in several political genealogies. For instance, Trump's populism hearkens back to the demagoguery of Huey Long, former governor of Louisiana, or Sidney Johnston Catts, the conspiracy-mongering Prohibition Party governor of Florida.[3] At the same time, Trump's attempt to translate business acumen into political power places him among the ranks of Herbert Hoover, Ross Perot, and, of course, Romney. In addition, commentators have attributed Trump's total takeover of the Republican Party to everything from the ubiquity of social media to the rise in white nationalist fervor to coastal elitism. There is truth in all of these things, to be sure. However, Trump has been remarkably consistent in his image over time, and the origins of that image are not fully political. Investigations into Trump's political precedents are important for what they reveal about America culturally and socially. However, if we are to understand the roots of Trump's appeal (positive and negative) to Americans I would argue that we need to examine the discourses, born out of the corporate culture of the 1980s, that allowed Trump to develop and construct himself as an image because it is these discourses that nourish and sustain Trump's particular brand of populist nationalism.

While Romney spoke and acted like a CEO, Trump speaks and acts like a corporation. Like that of a corporation, his use of language is generic and gestural, less concerned with communication and the conveyance of particular information, and more focused on creating impressions, managing others' orientations towards himself. Trump's lack of coherence, his prevarication, his supposed narcissism, all emerge from Trump's tendency to continually reconstruct himself in the present, revising and modifying views, histories, and interpretations to suit his present ends in much the same way that a corporation constructs itself in a continual present. The difference, of course, is that while the American public is accustomed to, even passively accepting of, this behavior from corporate entities, we initially find it jarring in what is ostensibly a biological human. At the same time, the infection of American culture with corporate culture and discourse means that corporate speech is legible to the vast majority of the American public. Romney's metonymic distinction between himself and his firm alienated voters who read him as elite and out of touch. Trump's collapse of the metonymic relationship between himself and his company, his insistence on speaking as though he were his company, however, renders him familiar, even comfortable. The difference is that the popular circulation of corporate culture has disciplined us to dismiss the inconsistency and mendaciousness of corporate discourse while reading into it our own desires.

## Popular Corporate Culture and Corporate Aesthetics

The proliferation of US popular corporate culture in the 1980s occurred as part of the naturalization of neoliberalism in the United States. According to David Harvey, the corporate managerial class, financiers, and politicians began coordinated efforts to implement a shift to neoliberalism in US culture and politics in the early 1970s (Harvey 43). In this book, I am following Wendy Brown's definition of neoliberalism as a kind of "rationality" that "disseminates the *model of the market* to all domains and activities—even where money is not at issue—and configures human beings exhaustively as market actors, always, only, and everywhere" (Brown 31). By disseminating neoliberal ideology throughout different levels of social and economic organization, pro-corporate forces generated a popular consensus that neoliberal market-based solutions were the most effective way to secure personal and national freedom (Harvey 42). This consensus ultimately led to pro-corporate forces "capturing" the Republican Party and successfully putting Ronald Reagan in the White House (Harvey 48). It is important to note that part of this process involved activating the latent political power of white evangelical Christians in the United States and forming an alliance between these voters and the Republicans (Harvey 49). As Harvey argues, however, the neoliberalization of the United States necessitated significant cultural shifts in order to support these political and economic changes (Harvey 42). What I am calling popular corporate culture, texts and discourses that speak to or about aspects of corporate life and circulate outside of the workplace, produces a hermeneutic that disciplines us to read and interpret corporate signification in sympathetic ways while promoting the integration of neoliberalism into our everyday lives. Here, we might think of texts like CEO autobiographies or popular management guides as well as corporate social media feeds and "business speak." Erica Schoenberger argues that CEO autobiographies work to "legitimize" the executive managerial class, through their representations, a mechanism I would argue extends to all popular corporate culture, though with a variety of objectives (Schoenberger 295–296). The production of popular corporate culture supports neoliberal conceptions of the individual, the state, and the firm, disciplining us to read the authoritarian and unequal power distributions within corporations as normative and to understand the intrusion of corporate discourses into our so-called private lives as acceptable, even desirable. This process legitimizes the viability of businessperson presidential candidates who promise to remake the American government and American life in the image of the American corporation. As neoliberalism has come to dominate social, economic, and political life in the United States, popular corporate culture has replaced our cultural narratives and the images with which we identify and through which we understand the world with the images and narratives of the corporation.

While management literature has existed since the nineteenth century, an expansion of mass-market production and dissemination of popular management books and other forms of popular corporate culture into mainstream US culture coincided with efforts to remake the United States along neoliberal lines in the 1970s and 1980s (Furusten 3). As cultural objects promoting corporate life and ideology proliferated, they developed what I will call corporate aesthetics, images, uses of language, narratives, forms, genres, and figures used to discipline us into pro-corporate discourse and to allow us to signal belonging to the greater corporate culture of the United States. From power ties to tiger teams to notions of "leadership," we have been socialized into the vocabularies and grammars of corporate life even if we do not or have not worked in a corporation per se. Recognizing corporate aesthetics as such is important because these aesthetics have filtered throughout US society and culture, offering systems of signification that may seem harmless or banal, but that facilitate neoliberalism's collapses of the distinctions between individual and firm, life and labor, private and public. While scholars like Lance Cummings have examined the ways in which Trump draws on evangelical Christian discourse and New Age discourses on language's power over the self to construct his Twitter persona, little attention has been paid to how the discourses of popular corporate culture inflect Trump's signification (Cummings 52–70). The discourses that Cummings identifies, New Age self-help books and evangelical Christian discourses influenced by self-help ideologies, share with popular corporate culture methods of commodification and circulation, particularly in the ways that all of these productions participate in the mainstreaming of neoliberal ideology in the United States.

One of the effects of the ascendency of the corporation in US culture is that corporate personhood has become the model for all personhood. As Brown argues, in neoliberal thought, "both persons and states are construed on the model of the contemporary firm," in that they seek to "maximize their capital value in the present and enhance their future value...through practices of entrepreneurialism, self-investment, and/or attracting investors" (Brown 22). According to Brown, neoliberalism remakes us as "human capital... [formulating] the subject as both a member of a firm and as itself a firm, and in both cases as appropriately conducted by the governance practices appropriate to firms" (Brown 34). As part of this process, we can see in the popularity and omnipresence of texts and discourses of self-help, productivity, and management how popular corporate culture has crossed the cell walls between the life of the firm and the life of the neoliberal subject as a firm, introducing managerial practices and concepts across all spheres.[4]

The neoliberal subject's accrual of corporate characteristics is not unidirectional, however. As Richard Hardack argues, we are caught in a "zero-sum game" in which corporations receive human characteristics such as "privacy, legal rights and exemptions, and traditional forms of continuity," while human beings become "more impersonal and generic, and increasingly defined by their relations to things" (Hardack 38). As neoliberal subjects leading increasingly generic lives focused on consumerism, our strategies for representing our lives and the heuristics by which we evaluate others' representations of their lives increasingly resemble strategies of corporate communication. We might think here of the kinds of life writing produced via social media, where one's online presence is curated to present images that fit the conventions of the particular platform and the expectations of one's audience. The blurring of distinctions between corporate and human life writing become more pronounced when we think of the interactions between corporations and humans in social media spaces. On Twitter, for instance, a human interlocuter might respond to an utterance made by a corporation and the corporation might respond to the human's interjection, both parties represented by identically formatted avatars, both constrained by the same character limit. As more of our lives play out on social media and through technological mediation, we not only become intuitive readers of corporate signification, we also begin to approach the autobiographical impulse through corporate methods.

Like human persons, corporations produce images and narratives of their lives or histories for public consumption. The stakes for this kind of corporate life writing are high—as artificial persons, corporations exist as assemblages, knowable through their property, exchanges, agents, processes, and discourse, but ultimately incorporeal. As a function of this fundamental absence or lack at the heart of a corporate entity, a corporation's agency and coherence must be produced through language that gives the corporation a unified voice to speak from and a narrative to connect together its many disparate entanglements. As Hardack argues, the agents of a corporation serve as "partial surrogates" and are not synonymous with the corporation itself, but "their external 'biographical' representations create the corporation...advertising and corporate autobiographies and biographies do not describe or correspond to existing 'persons,' but generate them" (Hardack 37). The generation of corporations through speech and text is a given to organizational scholars like Mario Burghausen and John M.T. Balmer who argue that corporations construct narratives of their past in accordance with the "changing circumstances, purposes, and interests in the [corporation's] present" (Burghausen 392). Some scholars like Agnes Delahaye et al. have pointed out that corporate narratives face generic pressures and audience expectations, much as any piece of life writing would.[5] I would note that part of the difference here is that a corporate narrative is always contingent on the present, generating an image of its agency that will be useful for its current goals. As a result, the narrative of a corporation's life need not remain consistent, but rather consistency emerges from the constant, present reiteration of the corporate person inflected by whatever narrative is currently most useful.

Autobiography has always been literary and rhetorical in the sense that any autobiographical account involves the imposition of outside editing and organization on a life in order to render that life in narrative form. The corporatization of human life, however, brings autobiographical practice closer to what I will refer to as life production. In his seminal essay on autobiography, Paul de Man writes,

> We assume that life produces the autobiography as an act produces its consequences, but can we not suggest, with equal justice, that the autobiographical project may itself produce and determine the life and that whatever the writer does is in fact governed by the technical demands of self-portraiture and thus determined, in all its aspects, by the resources of his medium? (De Man 69)

Under ideal circumstances (which, perhaps, never existed) autobiography would convey, transparently and faithfully, the narrative substance of a life as it was lived, collapsing as much as possible the distance between the writing subject and the reader. However, as de Man is suggesting here, the recognizable contours and the narrative structure of a life are imposed by "the autobiographical project," producing a "life" out of an otherwise undifferentiated mass of experiences. We might also read de Man's question here more literally. In the United States, as neoliberal subjects in a corporate culture, we are called upon at all points to produce our lives in certain ways. Across society, students, middle managers, academics, and parents cultivate activities, hobbies, projects, internships, even friendships and families, on the basis of how these lived experiences can be made legible on resumes, CVs, college applications, and social media. In many cases, we pursue our endeavors with the autobiographical project in mind, eschewing those activities that cannot be easily rendered or that do not provide a clear return on investment. As life production proceeds in tandem with the evolution of corporate personhood, our lives are increasingly networked and enframed, attached to products, services, brands, and technologies that render life production consumable and commodified.[6] Ultimately, even as corporations modify the tropes of genres like autobiography and history to construct their personhood, human beings have begun to construct our lives with these modified tropes, embodying ever more fully a firm-like subjectivity.

## Trump Life

While Donald Trump is ostensibly a real estate magnate turned politician, his actual life's work has been one long autobiographical project. The commodity that Trump pedals is his name and image. While Trump began by attaching his name to buildings, as his public visibility grew, Trump used his name to designate a wide range of products and services (Williams, Narayanswamy). Unlike other brands that share a name with their progenitor, like Ralph Lauren or Marc Jacobs, the signification of Trump's brand is generated by the life Trump produces for public consumption. At the core of Trump's life production are his three autobiographies, *TRUMP: The Art of the Deal* (1987), *TRUMP: Surviving at the Top* (later retitled *TRUMP: The Art of Survival*) (1990), and *TRUMP: The Art of the Comeback* (1997). *The Art of the Deal* establishes an image of Trump as an executive and a manager that is then reiterated in the subsequent books. Each of the books is either ghostwritten or coauthored and builds the signification of Trump's brand by insisting on his deal-making prowess, his wealth, and a version of his personality. The books, however, do not necessarily correspond with significant shifts or developments in Trump's lived experience.[7] Instead, after *The Art of the Deal*, the books extend and reiterate the initial image of Trump. For instance, in *Surviving at the Top*, Trump writes, "This is Phase Two of my life," suggesting on the surface a shift or movement, a noticeable break with what has come before (Trump *Surviving at the Top* 4). The book, however, borrows its aesthetics, structure, generic moves, and focuses from *The Art of the Deal*, producing a reiteration instead of a shift. The only real "Phase Two" of Trump's "life" in *Surviving at the Top* is that the book is his second autobiography, a move that implies Trump's life is coterminous with the boundaries of the texts. This blurring of life and life production continues as Trump takes the life produced in his autobiographies and transposes it to other mediums, like his stint as host of *The Apprentice* where he performed the kind of executive management his autobiographies detail or his ill-fated Trump University, premised on the deal-making and real estate knowhow the autobiographies claim Trump possesses. When Trump turned to politics, he did so through an extension of his life production apparatus, releasing *The America We Deserve* in 2000, *Time to Get Tough: Making America #1 Again* in 2011, and *Crippled America: How to Make America Great Again* in 2015 while maintaining a heavy, political Twitter presence. Each of these political books, as well as Trump's Twitter usage, employed an ethos founded in the life Trump produced in his earlier autobiographies, using his supposed business acumen to legitimate his claim to a right to speak about and participate in politics.

While Donald Trump, the biological human being, serves as the anchor to the life production done in his name, Trump exists more fully as an assemblage, operating under the logics of corporate speech and the influence of corporate aesthetics. Although he writes of earlier joint-stock companies, Henry Turner's description of the corporation as assemblages of "human and nonhuman things...all held together by many different points of translation," still pertains—corporations are aggregate, fictional beings, locatable through the material and discursive practices they encompass (Turner 104). While Trump serves as the face of his life production, he does not write his autobiographies himself, just as he may not compose all of his tweets himself.[8] Instead, like a corporation, he employs a range of surrogates to speak for him and a variety of signs to substitute for himself while laying claim to any speech made on his behalf. The Trump assemblage mirrors structurally the Trump Organization itself. In a letter addressed to Trump on in 2015, Sheri A. Dillon and William F. Nelson, two of Trump's tax attorneys, wrote,

> you hold interests as the sole or principal owner in approximately 500 separate entities. These entities are collectively referred to and do business as The Trump Organization...Because you operate these businesses almost exclusively through sole proprietorships and/or closely held partnerships, your personal federal income tax returns are inordinately large and complex for an individual. (Dillon, Nelson)

The Trump Organization, Trump's private company, is actually an assemblage of other companies, the name of the primary Organization standing in metonymically for the other companies, enabling an indefinite chain of substitutions. At the same time, these are "almost exclusively" structured as "sole proprietorships and/or closely held partnerships," indicating that the myriad companies that make up the Trump Organization are primarily run either by Trump directly or through collaboration with trusted individuals, possibly family.[9] Unlike a public corporation where shares are traded and shareholders participate in corporate governance, Trump's corporations are retained under his full control, an aspect of corporate structure that will be integral to Trump's life production. The collapse of the distance between the Trump Organization and Trump the human being is visible in the attorneys' note that the complexity of the Trump Organization's structure and how its businesses are operated causes Trump's "personal federal income tax returns" to be "inordinately large and complex for an individual." While the Trump Organization gathers together "approximately 500 separate entities" in one assemblage, the responsibility for and control of the assemblage reverts to Trump the individual.

Trump's position as the head of the Trump Organization allows him to subvert the logics of corporate speech to reinforce the production of his life as a successful businessperson. A key component of a corporation's assemblage that allows it to generate an image and narrative of itself is the special metonymic relationship between a CEO and an organization. Purnima Bose argues that the CEO "becomes a biographical metonym of corporate history, which necessarily truncates the complexity of [the corporation's] operations while offering consumers an easily packaged narrative about the company" (Bose 31). Laura Lyons argues, CEOs signify "a version of the corporation" that is, nonetheless, not quite the whole corporation, thereby "[creating] a potent alchemy of identification and disidentification that usually allows contemporary corporations to have it all ways" (Lyons 102). In her discussion of Tony Hayward, the CEO and spokesman for BP during the oil spill of 2010, Lyons demonstrates that one of the basic moves of CEO-centered corporate speech allows the CEO to speak for (and thereby as) the corporation while also retaining some degree of individuality. According to Lyons, one of Hayward's problems was that he did not successfully manage the metonymic relationship between firm and executive, speaking for himself at times he was expected to speak for the company (Lyons 96–97). Trump's life production manipulates these metonymic relationships, substituting Trump the human CEO for Trump the corporation at various points while also using the mask of the Trump Organization to reduce Trump's personal liability and accountability. Trump's life production also represents an intensification of the "biographical metonym," on an aesthetic level, using Trump's celebrity lifestyle and gauche personal aesthetic to build the signification of the Trump assemblage. As a result, the distance between Trump and his Organization collapses, the actions of one coterminous with the other.

Trump's collapse of the usual metonymies of corporate speech allows him to figure himself as the ideal neoliberal subject, a key component of his populist appeal. Trump performs neoliberal subjectivity by going beyond simply managing his life like a corporation and instead actively merging his life with that of the Trump Organization to the point that the two are indistinguishable. While it is the legal fiction of the corporation as a non-human person that allows Trump access to the kinds of liability protections and financial structures that make his real estate development possible, Trump's identification with his Organization allows him to produce his life in such a way that he personally claims credit and, crucially, receives credit from the public for his Organization's actions. In particular, Trump's conflation of his human and corporate persons allows him to more fully embody neoliberalism's fetishization of "individual freedom in the marketplace" while intensifying his performance of the neoliberal virtues of competition and individual responsibility (Harvey 53). As Trump writes in *Surviving at the Top*, "If someone is going around labeling people winners and losers, I want to play the game and, of course, come out on the right side," a statement he underscores shortly thereafter by writing, "my main purpose in life is to keep winning" (Trump *Surviving at the Top*

5,13). Here, Trump reduces life and business to a binary between winning and losing, underscoring the moral dimension of wealth in neoliberal thought—if you have it, you are morally good; if you don't, you are suspect.[10] Under this rubric, moves that would otherwise seem ethically problematic become virtuous. For instance, in the September 26, 2016 presidential debate, in response to Secretary of State Hillary Clinton's accusation that Trump was hiding his tax returns to avoid revealing that he had not owed federal income text, Trump interjected, "That makes me smart" (Mangan). While Clinton attempted to tie tax paying to civic duty, pointing out that in paying no taxes, Trump would not have paid towards the support of troops or schools, Trump projected a neoliberal position that any move to maximize individual wealth was admirable and preferable. This position is in line with Trump's descriptions of his business practices across his life production where he endeavors to reduce his personal financial risk as much as possible (Trump *Art of the Deal* 146). Trump would not be able to perform these intensified acts of neoliberal subjectivity without the Trump assemblage, but he also would not be able to claim these acts to bolster his political profile without collapsing the distance between himself and his firm. In order to reinforce this performance, Trump has developed consistent aesthetic principles that govern his life production across his assemblage.

*Trumpian Aesthetics*

Integral to the signification of the Trump assemblage and indebted to corporate aesthetics, Trump's personal aesthetics value reproducibility, consistency, and attention to surfaces over other concerns. For instance, a commonly remarked on idiosyncrasy of Trump's is his McDonald's order: two fish fillets, two Big Macs, and a Diet Coke (Desantis). Explaining his preference, Trump said, "I'm a very clean person. I like cleanliness, and I think you're better off going [to McDonald's] than maybe someplace that you have no idea where the food's coming from...It's a certain standard. I think the food's good" (Desantis). For Trump, what matters is not the quality of the food, though he does think it's "good," but rather the consistency of the food, that it's prepared to "a certain standard." The same principle drives Trump's sartorial choices. Trump's suits are Brioni, an expensive Italian brand, but Trump tailors them unusually, preferring baggy, seemingly ill-fitting cuts (Green). In addition, he usually wears an overlong, often red tie that hangs below his waist. Recognizable and reproducible, Trump's suits exaggerate executive fashion, emphasizing those elements that symbolize power and success, the power tie, the designer suit. While the presentation would seem grotesque or strange on another individual, a mark of a lack of taste or a failure to understand social codes, Trump's consistent repetition of the suit and its subsequent association with his persona normalizes it. The same principle undergirds the ubiquitous red Make America Great Again (MAGA) hats. As an object in isolation, the hat appears cheap and minimal, like a rapidly produced promotional item for a business. Indeed, the hat lacks a campaign logo or the candidate's name, mainstays of political campaign apparel. Through repetition and association, however, the hat accrues symbolic value beyond its physical appearance. Like Trump's name on his hotels and products, the MAGA hat relies on reproducibility to yoke its wearer up to Trump's assemblage. This move is underscored by Trump's routine wearing of the hat himself. In effect, the wearer of the hat becomes a simulacrum of Trump, assuming his characteristics and associations while shedding their own.

Another example of Trump's metastatic proliferation appears in a campaign ad for the then Florida Republican gubernatorial candidate Ron DeSantis in 2018. The ad begins with an image of DeSantis' wife, Casey, declaring that "everyone knows" that "Ron DeSantis is endorsed by President Trump," a declaration reinforced by a text caption reading, "Casey DeSantis/Ron DeSantis Endorsed by Trump." Casey DeSantis goes on to declare that "Ron is an amazing dad," leading into a series of vignettes in which DeSantis plays with, reads to, and teaches his child by parroting aspects of Trump's life production. Building with blocks, DeSantis tells his child to "build the wall"; ostensibly reading *The Art of the Deal* to his child, DeSantis recalls Trump's *Apprentice* tagline, "You're fired" (a line that does not appear in the book); DeSantis teaches his child to read by slowly pointing through the phrase "Make America Great Again" on a Trump yard sign; finally, DeSantis recites the Trumpism "Bigly—so good," while looking down at a baby wearing a MAGA onesie ("Ron DeSantis Has Released An Ad Indoctrinating His Children Into Trumpism"). Casey DeSantis ends the commercial by saying, "People say Ron is all Trump, but he's so much more." However, in the ad, other than to say, "I love that part" when reading *The Art of the Deal*, DeSantis only speaks Trump's words. Indeed, the ad constructs DeSantis' fatherhood as a Trumpian metastasis, DeSantis, overwritten by Trump, teaching his children to parrot Trump as well. The ad contains no reference to DeSantis' own policies or even to any political issue specific to Florida, instead absorbing DeSantis into Trump's assemblage. The argument the ad makes is not that DeSantis is politically similar to Trump, but that to vote for DeSantis is to vote for Trump, even going so far as to reuse Trump's campaign merchandise as props while failing to include any DeSantis campaign branding. As a result, DeSantis is subsumed, reduced to a reflection in the mirrored façade of Trump's life production.

Trump's personal aesthetics and their metastatic reproduction dovetail with populist aesthetics in their insistence that the metonymies of corporate signification can be collapsed to a single surface. In broad terms, populism is a form of politics where a politician (or representative) claims to represent an "authentic" definition of "the people" against the figure of "an elite" that works against the people's interests (Espejo 98). In this way, populism is, as Paulina Ochoa Espejo describes, "an ideology of collective identity" that builds its cohesion through "exclusion" (Espejo 94). For instance, right-wing populism usually includes, alongside representations of "the elite," the figuration of an Other who is less-than or inferior to the people (Voelz 204). Johannes Voelz argues that right-wing populism develops an aesthetics in order to manage the production of the illusion that the distance between representative and represented has been eliminated successfully. Voelz sees campaign rallies, like Trump's, as the site in contemporary politics where the "performative acts" of representation generate an "imaginary experience of unity and communion," between the representative and the represented (Voelz 206,209). These communions, however, are never complete and are unsustainable, because they "are momentary effects of dynamic relations" predicated on "the continuing non-identity of those involved in the performance" (Voelz 209). While Voelz sees the performance of populist representation at the political rally as the center of populist aesthetics, Espejo argues convincingly that populism relies on the construction of the represented as a "people," a group with boundaries and a sense of sovereignty bound together by "shared aesthetic judgments about cultural matters" (Espejo 95). If we take Hardack's point that corporate personhood has impoverished human personhood, rendering humans more "generic," and consider the role of media technology, like social media, in twenty-first-century life production, we can see how the kind of communion and identification integral to the political rally manifests online as a pooling of aesthetic resources for the construction of an exclusive people (Hardack 38). As Michele Lockhart argues, we are in a "new age of rhetoric" where social media contributes to a destabilization of truth and reality, a destabilization of which Trump takes advantage (Lockhart 4). Trump's use of Twitter and the Trump assemblage's use of memes and rapidly produced consumer goods allow Trump supporters to substitute Trump's voice, image, and ideas for their own as they share tweets and memes and produce content that indicates that they "share" the "aesthetic judgments" of the people Trump claims to represent.

Trump is able to tap into this populist appeal because of the structural similarities between populist and corporate aesthetics. Both populist and corporate aesthetics operate through manipulations of the rhetorical figures of metonymy and prosopopoeia. Metonymy substitutes the whole for the part or the part for the whole, driving the logics by which a CEO may speak for a corporation or a populist representative may construct and speak on behalf of a people.[11] Prosopopoeia points to the construction of a face or mask, the fiction of a unified speaking position concretized in the "we" of corporate or populist speech.[12] The narratives of populist and corporation formations both rely on the construction of inclusive and exclusive principles. Where the populist people is constructed against excluded Others, the corporate body is constructed against competitors, market forces, and consumers. In both cases, the collective predicates its identity on a reaction against outside agents that are figured prosopopoetically as cohesive actors, like "the media" and "the market." These formal sympathies are not accidental. Neoliberalism's cooptation of discourses of individual freedom draws on populist formations to construct the neoliberal subject as a corporation in miniature. For instance, Purnima Bose notes that one of the rhetorical shifts that accompanied General Electric's public embrace of vampire capitalism is the shift from the phrase "lifetime employment" to "lifetime employability" (Bose 54). As a market actor, the neoliberal subject must always be ready to join a new organization and organizations, themselves market actors, need not feel any obligation to retain employees. As a result of the rise of this ideology in the 1980s, popular corporate culture proliferated as management became a lifestyle rather than a job. CEOs, as the emblems of what Bose calls "entrepreneurial individualism," become models of subjectivity, the individuals who have most successfully cultivated their personal investments while combating the market forces of economic, social, and political life. The crucial bridge that allowed Trump and, to a lesser extent, Ross Perot to translate their business success into populist politics where candidates like Mitt Romney or Carly Fiorina failed is entrepreneurial individualism's juxtaposition of the heroic CEO and what Bose calls "the corporation as an ailing entity" (Bose 55). By constructing the corporation as ailing, the entrepreneurial individualist can emphasize her acumen and prowess, fighting against outside forces to restore order and prosperity. Trump routinely constructs the United States "as an ailing entity" that only he, the heroic manager, can save. On the surface, such an argument would seem absurd, but it resonates with deeply embedded cultural narratives that we have come to take for granted.

The 1980s popular corporate culture is rife with populist and nationalist rhetoric aimed at naturalizing neoliberal thought in the social, political, and economic life of the United States. As I will argue, we must consider that this discourse, commodified and circulated in a number of forms in which Trump participates, informs Trump's development of populist and nationalist ideas. Scholars have generally not taken Trump's business experience and participation in the 1980s corporate management culture seriously, an oversight that I would argue occludes a major influence on Trump's self-presentation and speech. As I will argue in the following pages, Trump's life production, from his autobiographies, to his political books, to his presidential responses to national crises, bears marks of the corporate management culture of the long 1980s.[13] An examination of the influence of popular management culture on Trump's meaning making will demonstrate the degree to which neoliberal cultural forms have allowed Trump's rise to power by distorting, overwriting, and manipulating the signifying strategies of corporate America.

Chapter 2 examines how Trump's *The Art of the Deal* distorts and overwrites the genres of the CEO autobiography and popular management book in order to legitimate Trump's position in the executive managerial class. CEO autobiographies and popular management books are key components of popular corporate culture, providing a ready means of naturalizing corporate conceptions of power and authority in American culture. Trump's *Art of the Deal* appears in 1987, part of the inundation of CEO autobiographies in the long 1980s. Trump's book borrows generic markers from other texts, rehearsing gestures that, on the surface, appear to fit standard narratives of the CEO's relationship to the firm. However, Trump, CEO of a private company where distinctions between CEO and firm do not apply, undermines key distinctions between manager and company. The chapter examines *Art of the Deal*'s manipulation of temporality, narrative resolution, and generic conventions in order to understand how the text produces Trump as a member managerial class. Where other popular corporate texts translate corporate organizations of authority and power into political and cultural spheres, the chapter argues that Trump's text simulates management, collapsing the careful negotiation of the CEO-Firm relationship inherent to CEO autobiographies and popular management books in order to present Trump as a heroic manager. In the end, the chapter argues that Trump intuits that the role of CEO in the public imaginary is not connected to an actual position or work experience, but rather inheres in a series of gestures, like the CEO autobiography, that exist outside of any particular responsibilities or achievements. Ultimately, the chapter makes the case that the importance of *The Art of the Deal* lies in its status as an object, in how it signifies and circulates on its surface, rather than in its contents, suggesting that the rhetorical goal of popular management books is not to provide means for managing, but rather to offer the illusion that there is a justifiable rationale for corporate organizations of power.

Chapter 3 examines Donald Trump's autobiographical debt to Lee Iacocca, whose 1984 *Autobiography* set the standard for 1980s CEO memoirs. Iacocca produces himself as a heroic manager for the American public by dramatizing popular corporate discourse about Japanese competition. Amid the US trade war with Japan, numerous popular management books appeared, supporting neoliberal reforms to corporate life by arguing that Japan would soon displace the United States as an economic superpower if drastic measures were not taken. Iacocca uses this discourse to construct a virtual politics in his essay, "Make America Great Again," a politics that resembles political discourse, but which is not intended to be enacted. Iacocca uses the essay to feint at running for president, opening a space in the American imaginary for a populist, neoliberal business candidate who seems to tell it like it is. The chapter turns to Trump's second autobiography *Surviving at the Top* to show how Trump builds on the images and politics Iacocca articulates while also engaging with Japanese competition discourse. Trump capitalizes on Iacocca's innovations, aesthetically and politically, to produce himself as a concerned businessman with the toughness to turn America around. Ultimately, the chapter argues that part of the appeal of pretend candidacies like Iacocca and Trump lies in their claim that they would never be acceptable as candidates.

Chapter 4 contextualizes Trump's three campaign policy books: *The America We Deserve, Time to Get Tough*, and *Crippled America* within developments in twenty-first-century campaign autobiography. The chapter argues that popular corporate culture has infected and financialized the American marketplace of political representations. As the frequency in the publication of mass-market campaign memoirs increases and these books garner sales, candidates increasingly run for office in order to sell books, generating economic and social capital at the same time. By playing the futures market of US politics, floating candidacies, and publishing books to capitalize on voter anticipation, candidates embrace the strategy of Iacocca and Trump as the norm. The chapter examines autobiographies by candidates who branded themselves as business candidates, arguing that Mitt Romney, Herman Cain, and Carly Fiorina failed to match Trump's electoral success because they worked too hard to produce themselves as legitimate politicians. The chapter then turns to Trump's books to demonstrate how, over the course of two decades, Trump constructs himself as a heroic manager who can solve America's ills, contributing to a discourse that radically reimagines the presidency.

The book's coda, Chapter 5, uses images of the Capitol Insurrection and Trump's departure from office to think about the influence of corporate culture on United States' political life production. The chapter argues that the Capitol rioters, awash in digital media, lose their subjecthood to become pure product and production, producing Trump even as he produces them. The chapter considers the ways in which Trump encourages emulation of his life producing repertoire, even though that life production is largely an emulation itself. Ultimately, the chapter argues that Trump's signature is the appropriation and erasure of signatures themselves.

## Notes

1 For instance: Martinez, Gina. "President Trump Makes Baseless Claim That Voters Change Clothes to Cast Multiple Votes," *Time*, 14 Nov. 2018.
2 For an account of how political opponents treated Romney's relationship with Bain, see: Borchers, Tyler and Jerry L. Miller, "Bain & Political Capital in the 2012 GOP Primary Debates," *American Behavioral Scientist*, vol. 58, no. 4 (2014): 574–590.
3 On Long, see: Ostiguy, Pierre and Kenneth M. Roberts. "Putting Trump in Comparative Perspective: Populism and Politicization of the

Sociocultural Low," *Brown Journal of World Affairs*, vol. XXIII, no. 1 (2016): 25–50. On Catts, see: Flynt, Wayne. *Cracker Messiah: Governor Sidney J. Catts of Florida*. Louisiana State University Press, 1977.
4 For an example, see the work of Melissa Gregg on the proliferation of productivity literature: Gregg, Melissa. *Counterproductive: Time Management in the Knowledge Economy*. Duke University Press, 2018.
5 See: Delahaye, Agnès and Charles Booth, Peter Clark, Stephen Procter, and Michael Rowlinson, "The Genre of Corporate History," *Journal of Organizational Change Management*, vol. 22, no. 1 (2009): 27–48.
6 See, for example: Smith, Sidonie and Julia Watson. "Virtually Me: A Toolbox about Online Self-Presentation," *Life Writing in the Long Run: A Smith & Watson Autobiography Studies Reader*. Michigan Publishing Services, 2016.
7 *The Art of the Comeback* corresponds with Trump's rebound from divorce and bankruptcy, but is itself part of his "comeback," a money-making endeavor that signifies his return to equilibrium, rather than a mere chronicle of personal disaster.
8 Especially early on in the Trump administration, there were clear signs that at least one staffer composed some of Trump's tweets. See: Feinberg, Ashley. "How to Tell When Someone Else Tweets from @realDonaldTrump." *Wired*, 6 Oct. 2017.
9 See: Majaski, Christina. "Private vs. Public Company: What's the Difference?" *Investopedia*, 11 Jul. 2019.
10 Neoliberalism's morality of wealth may help to explain the amount of Trump's life production dedicated to reassuring readers that he is wealthy and recovered quickly from his bankruptcies. For instance, in *The Art of the Comeback*.
11 See: "Metonymy," *Princeton Encyclopedia of Poetry and Poetics*, edited by Alex Preminger, Princeton University Press, 1975: 499–500.
12 See: de Man, Paul. "Autobiography as De-Facement," *The Rhetoric of Romanticism*. Columbia University Press, 1984: 76.
13 Leigh Claire La Berge coins the term "the Long 1980s" in: La Berge, Leigh Claire. *Scandals and Abstraction: Financial Fiction of the Long 1980s*. Oxford University Press, 2015.

## Works Cited

Borchers, Tyler and Jerry L. Miller. "Bain & Political Capital in the 2012 GOP Primary Debates." *American Behavioral Scientist*, vol. 58, no. 4, 2014, pp. 574–590.

Bose, Purnima. "General Electric, Corporate Personhood, and the Emergence of the Professional Manager." *Cultural Critique and the Global Corporation*, edited by Purnima Bose and Laura Lyons, Indiana University Press, 2010, pp. 28–63.

Brown, Wendy. *Undoing the Demos: Neoliberalism's Stealth Revolution*. MIT University Press, 2015.

Burghausen, Mario and John M.T. Balmer, "Repertoires of the Corporate Past: Explanation and Framework. Introducing an Integrated and

Dynamic Perspective." *Corporate Communications*, vol. 19, no. 4, 2014, pp. 384–402.

Cummings, Lance. "The Dark Alchemy of Donald Trump: Re-Inventing Presidential Rhetorics through Christian and 'New Age' Discourses." *President Donald Trump and His Political Discourse: Ramifications of Rhetoric via Twitter*, edited by Michele Lockhart, Routledge, 2019, pp. 52–70.

Delahaye, Agnès and Charles Booth, Peter Clark, Stephen Procter, and Michael Rowlinson. "The Genre of Corporate History." *Journal of Organizational Change Management*, vol. 22, no. 1, 2009, pp. 27–48.

De Man, Paul. *The Rhetoric of Romanticism*. Columbia University Press, 1984.

Desantis, Rachel. "Donald Trump's Lifelong Love of Fast Food, from His 2002 McDonald's Commercial to 'Hamberders." *New York Daily News*, 15 Jan. 2019, nydailynews.com/news/politics/ny-news-donald-trump-has-always-loved-fast-food-20190115-story.html.

Dillon, Sheri A., and William F. Nelson. "Re: Status of U.S. Federal Income Tax Returns." *Letter from Morgan Lewis and Bockius LLC*, 7 Mar. 2016, assets.donaldjtrump.com/Tax_Doc.pdf.

Dwyer, Devin. "Elizabeth Warren Slams Mitt Romney." *ABC News*, 26 Jun. 2012, abcnews.go.com/blogs/politics/2012/06/elizabeth-warren-slams-mitt-romney/.

Espejo, Paulina Ochoa. "Populism and the People." *Theory & Event*, vol. 20, no. 1, 2017, pp. 92–99.

Feinberg, Ashley. "How to Tell When Someone Else Tweets from @realDonaldTrump." *Wired*, 6 Oct. 2017, wired.com/story/tell-when-someone-else-tweets-from-realdonaldtrump/.

Flynt, Wayne. *Cracker Messiah: Governor Sidney J. Catts of Florida*. Louisiana State University Press, 1977.

Furusten, Staffan. *Popular Management Books: How They are Made and What They Mean for Organisations*. Routledge, 1999.

Green, Dennis. "Here's Why Donald Trump's Suits Look Cheap Even Though They Cost Thousands of Dollars." *Business Insider*, 4 Nov. 2016, businessinsider.com/why-donald-trumps-suits-look-cheap-2016-11.

Gregg, Melissa. *Counterproductive: Time Management in the Knowledge Economy*. Duke University Press, 2018.

Hardack, Richard. "New and Improved: The Zero-Sum Game of Corporate Personhood." *Biography*, vol. 27, no. 1, 2014, pp. 36–68.

Harvey, David. *A Brief History of Neoliberalism*. Oxford University Press, 2005.

Time Staff. "Here's Donald Trump's Presidential Announcement Speech." *Time*, 16 Jun. 2015, time.com/3923128/donald-trump-announcement-speech/.

Krieg, Gregory. "14 of Trump's Most Outrageous 'Birther' Claims—Half from after 2011." *CNN*, 16 Sep. 2016, cnn.com/2016/09/09/politics/donald-trump-birther/index.html.

La Berge, Leigh C. *Scandals and Abstraction: Financial Fiction of the Long 1980s*. Oxford University Press, 2015.
Lockhart, Michele. "Introduction." *President Donald Trump and His Political Discourse: Ramifications of Rhetoric via Twitter*, edited by Michele Lockhart, Routledge, 2019, pp. 1–10.
Lyons, Laura. "'I'd Like My Life Back': Corporate Personhood and the BP Oil Disaster." *Biography*, vol. 34, no. 1, 2011, pp. 96–107.
Majaski, Christina. "Private vs. Public Company: What's the Difference?" *Investopedia*, 11 Jul. 2019, investopedia.com/ask/answers/difference-between-publicly-and-privately-held-companies/.
Mangan, Dan. "Trump Brags about Not Paying Taxes: 'That Makes Me Smart." *CNBC*, 26 Sep. 2016, cnbc.com/2016/09/26/trump-brags-about-not-paying-taxes-that-makes-me-smart.html.
Martinez, Gina. "President Trump Makes Baseless Claim That Voters Change Clothes to Cast Multiple Votes." *Time*, 14 Nov. 2018, time.com/5455294/trump-new-voter-fraud-allegations-change-clothes/.
Evans, Robert O. "Metonymy." *Princeton Encyclopedia of Poetry and Poetics*, Second Edition, edited by Alex Preminger, Princeton University Press, 1975, pp. 499–500.
Mikkelson, David. "Donald Trump's 'Nuclear' Speech." *Snopes*, 17 Aug. 2016, snopes.com/fact-check/donald-trump-sentence/.
Nader, Ralph. "Mitt Romney: A Corporation Masquerading as a Person for President." *Common Dreams*, 20 Sep. 2012, commondreams.org/views/2012/09/20/mitt-romney-corporation-masquerading-person-president.
Oliphant, James. "Romney in Iowa: 'Corporations Are People' Too." *Los Angeles Times*, 11 Aug. 2011, www.latimes.com/la-xpm-2011-aug-11-la-pn-romney-state-fair-20110811-story.html.
Ostiguy, Pierre and Kenneth M. Roberts. "Putting Trump in Comparative Perspective: Populism and Politicization of the Sociocultural Low." *Brown Journal of World Affairs*, vol. 23, no. 1, 2016, pp. 25–50.
Guardian News. "Ron DeSantis Has Released an Ad Indoctrinating His Children into Trumpism." *YouTube*, uploaded by Guardian News, 2 Aug. 2018, youtube.com/watch?v=z1YP_zZJFXs.
Sargent, Greg. "Mitt Romney: 'Corporations Are People." *The Washington Post*, 11 Aug. 2011, washingtonpost.com/blogs/plum-line/post/mitt-romney-corporations-are-people/2011/03/03/gIQA8Pjy8I_blog.html.
Schoenberger, Erica. "Corporate Autobiographies: The Narrative Strategies of Corporate Strategists." *Journal of Economic Geography*, vol. 1, 2001, pp. 277–298.
Smith, Sidonie and Julia Watson. "Virtually Me: A Toolbox about Online Self-Presentation." *Life Writing in the Long Run: A Smith & Watson Autobiography Studies Reader*, Michigan Publishing Services, 2016, pp. 225–260.

"Transcript: Donald Trump's Taped Comments about Women." *The New York Times*, 8 Oct. 2016, nytimes.com/2016/10/08/us/donald-trump-tape-transcript.html.

Trump, Donald and Charles Leerhsen. *Surviving at the Top*. Random House, 1990.

Trump, Donald J. and Tony Schwartz. *Art of the Deal*. First Edition. Random House, 1987.

Turner, Henry S. *The Corporate Commonwealth: Pluralism and Political Fictions in England, 1616–1651*. University of Chicago Press, 2016.

Voelz, Johannes. "Towards an Aesthetics of Populism, Part I: The Populist Space of Appearance." *Yearbook of Research in English and American Literature (REAL)*, vol. 34, 2018, pp. 203–228.

Williams, Aaron and Anu Narayanswamy. "How Trump Has Made Millions by Selling His Name." *Washington Post*, 25 Jan. 2017, https://www.washingtonpost.com/graphics/world/trump-worldwide-licensing/.

# 2 A Genius Purely by Instinct
## Simulating Management in *The Art of the Deal*

In his speech announcing his candidacy for the 2016 presidential election, Donald J. Trump stood in the atrium of Trump Tower and claimed, "our country needs a truly great leader, and we need a truly great leader now. We need a leader that wrote *The Art of the Deal*." The assertion comes at a turning point in the speech, as Trump turns from a litany of problems he claims America faces, to a description of his own potential strengths as a candidate. By positioning *The Art of the Deal* in this way, as the foundation of his construction of himself as a candidate, Trump seems to imply two things: that his authorship of *The Art of the Deal* is unproblematic and that *The Art of the Deal* contains a theory or methodology by which someone might effect change. Over the following years, *The Art of the Deal*'s co-writer, Tony Schwartz, would challenge the first of these claims, asserting that Trump had little patience for the usual processes of collaboration, forcing Schwartz to compose most of the text without Trump's direct input (Mayer). Trump responded through a spokesperson that he "was the source of all of the material in the Book and the inspiration for every word in the Book," threatening Schwartz with legal action (Mayer). While Trump stops short of the claim in his candidacy announcement that he "wrote *The Art of the Deal*," his response to Schwartz tethers the text to Trump, positioning himself as the generative force that made the text possible.

The text not only constructs Trump as he wants to be seen, it also serves as a primer of Trumpian aesthetics and ethos in miniature. At the same time, for Trump's purposes, his participation (or lack thereof) in the process of constructing the text's manuscript is unimportant. As with most of Trump's signification, once the book appears under the sign of his name, the text becomes his, part of the assemblage that produces and locates Trump in the world. The nature of *The Art of the Deal* has been misunderstood, however, thereby masking our understanding of what it contributes to Trump's life production. While some treat the text as a typical CEO autobiography, focusing on how the text presents a narrative of Trump's life, others, including Trump himself at times, treat the text as a kind of popular management book, a how-to guide for burnishing one's own deal-making artistry. As I will show in this chapter, neither of these things are completely true. Despite *The Art of the Deal*'s engagement with both of these genres, the text itself rejects both the sense of development and the practical implementation of theory that these genres require.

Examining *The Art of the Deal* at the intersection of life-writing studies and critical corporate studies allows us to recover the way the text manipulates the legibility of certain corporate genres in order to access and redefine political authority. Published in 1989, *The Art of the Deal* emerged in the midst of a historical moment saturated in popular books about corporate life. While CEO autobiographies and popular management books have existed in various forms since the late nineteenth century, the 1980s and 1990s saw massive acceleration in the production and consumption of these texts. *The Art of the Deal* draws on the legitimizing and symbolizing power of popular corporate culture to construct Trump as a member of the executive managerial class. In the process, however, *The Art of the Deal* distorts these corporate modes of signification to construct Trump as a version of the heroic CEO, but one who collapses, rather than draws, distinctions between himself and his firm.

As Erica Schoenberger argues, CEO autobiographies work "to establish the legitimacy" of the executive managerial class in the public sphere, by demonstrating that CEOs "have a right to the power [the autobiographies] represent [them] as wielding" (Schoenberger 296). For instance, Jack Welch's *Jack: Straight from the Gut* narrates Welch's success in leadership at General Electric in order to legitimize Welch's power over the hundreds of thousands of employees directly affected by his decisions.[1] Donald Trump, however, does not exist in quite the same corporate world as Welch. As the CEO of a private company, Trump was not in danger of being fired by a higher ranking executive or answerable to a board or even shareholders. When Michael Bloomberg called Trump a "pretend CEO," he was pointing to the fact that Trump's accountability as an executive was less complex than what a typical public corporation CEO would experience and that this lack of accountability undermines Trump's claims to legitimacy as a member of the executive managerial class (Gestalter).

Part of the work of *The Art of the Deal*, then, is not only to legitimize Trump's social position and power, but to construct Trump as a member of the executive managerial class in order to lay claim to the authority that such membership provides in American society. As a result, a significant portion of the framing of *The Art of the Deal* focuses on staging Trump as an executive who does executive work, primarily making decisions. In this way, Trump assumes the role of the heroic manager, a figure within an organization who single-handedly makes the managerial decisions that lead to the organization's success. One of the functions of management in general and the heroic manager specifically is to provide a representation or locus that legitimizes decision-making within an organization (Mayr and Siri 174). The heroic manager, as a decider, stabilizes the decision-making process of an organization by serving both as someone who makes decisions (thereby legitimizing a decision as a decision) and whose decisions are decisive (thus legitimizing the decidedness of a decision in the presence of alternatives). Where public CEOs can point to organizational decisions that are historically legible and narrate those decisions to demonstrate their managerial prowess, *The Art of the Deal* must first establish that Trump makes consequential decisions in the first place. The difficulty the text faces in demonstrating Trump's decision-making is that, unlike a car manufacturer or a computer technology company who produce products familiar and visible to a large number of Americans, the main product of the Trump Organization is Trump's name and the aura it carries. Without a tangible product, it is as easy to assume that Donald Trump makes no consequential decisions as it is to assume that he does. As a result, the text opens with Trump asserting that "Deals are my art form. Other people paint beautifully on canvas or write wonderful poetry. I like making deals, preferably big deals," locating the work of Trump as executive in the process of "making deals," suggesting that it is not the particular physical buildings or franchises that signify Trump's accomplishments (though the text does celebrate them), but rather the means by which these projects were realized (Trump *Art of the Deal* 3).

Both CEO autobiography and popular management books rely on a genre of management, the heroic manager, to construct their representations and effects. The heroic manager is a representation of a manager who can move throughout an organization, performing the work of any number of roles in order to solve single-handedly the organization's problems. The heroic manager is not, however, an embodiment of a coherent management theory, but rather a cultural construction of how a manager should manage. According to David L. Bradford and Allan R. Cohen, the heroic manager is driven by a "sense of centrality and responsibility" to make decisions and control subordinates in order to achieve success for the organization (Bradford and Cohen 31). Implicit in Bradford and Cohen's early description is the heroic manager's role in maintaining hierarchies within the organization, directing and enforcing vertical flows of power. Heroic management is not a complete theory of management because it does not answer what Mintzberg identifies as a crucial question: what does a manager do? (Mintzberg 3). Instead, the heroic manager reduces management to a single surface—the interface of manager and managed. The individual and firm become one synonymous figure. While this reinforces the authoritarian nature of corporate power by seemingly locating corporate agency in the actions of certain individuals, the refusal of metonymy by the heroic manager undermines the networks through which this power is distributed and the processes through which the organization reaches decisions.

This construction is metastatic, spreading throughout management studies, corporate culture, and the broader cultural imaginary, affecting how we understand management and how media represents management. In management studies, scholars have identified the heroic manager and argued against it at least since the early 1970s.[2] Even in the same year, 1984, that Lee Iacocca's *Iacocca: An Autobiography* became a best-seller based on an image of a kind of heroic manager, scholars like David L. Bradford and Allan R. Cohen connected the heroic manager to a cultural desire for heroes and recommend adopting "a postheroic model of management" (Bradford and Cohen 58). Other scholars like Robert Chia, Olga Ivanova, and Sybille Persson point to the ways that the image of the heroic manager persists well into the twenty-first century despite its impracticability.[3] Indeed, as Bernd Carsten Stahl reminds us, the heroic manager is still the predominant view of management in business schools and society (Stahl 106). Part of the heroic manager's appeal and conceptual resilience lies in its symbolizing effects. In a world dominated by corporate influence, the heroic manager, often figured as an idiosyncratic CEO or spokesperson, absorbs our uncertainty, giving a human face and origin to corporate agency and power. As Stahl argues, however, the heroic manager is not a role that a human can actually occupy, since the confluence of requisite qualities is unlikely to occur in a single individual (Stahl 107). Rather, the heroic manager functions metonymically, like the CEO, a part that stands in for the whole of the corporation at crucial junctures. Indeed, the ubiquity of the fiction of the heroic manager is what allows CEOs to serve as clearinghouses for corporate narrative; we are predisposed to look for a central manager whose influence and guiding hand can be felt in all parts of an organization as part of how we understand a corporation's actions.

While the life production of most CEOs uses images of heroic management, these images are deployed carefully as part of the negotiation of the metonymic relationship between CEO and firm. The CEO might take heroic action at a critical juncture, becoming the face of a particular innovation or crisis, but the collective figure of the corporation, a gestural "we," will emerge as well. It is this tension between the manager's management of resources and labor and management of shareholder and board member expectations that figures management in this discourse. Trump's business in an assemblage of private companies lacks these tensions. Most of his resources are financial, and the labor is contracted out. There are no shareholders or board members to appease. As a result, a narrative of Trump's business cannot produce Trump as a manager, denying him access to the social capital that position provides. To solve this representational problem, Trump effaces distinction between himself and company in order to appear managerial, to simulate the role of a CEO, circulating *The Art of the Deal* as though it were a management guide to simulate managerial expertise. However, this simulation produces an emphasis on the present and on simultaneity and demonstrates a lack of the emotional or personal growth a CEO autobiography typically narrates. Instead, like a corporation, Trump just expands, increasing his surface and his scope.

### Aesthetics of *The Art of the Deal*

*The Art of the Deal* produces Trump's life by avoiding the appearance of mediation or affectation. The text is not so much realistic, in that it attempts to faithfully convey a particular reality, as it is anti-poetic. There are almost no metaphors or similes in the text and little imagery. The text avoids dialogue for the most part and what affective language used is rudimentary. An examination of one of the more descriptive passages of the text that contains the text's only explicit reference to poetic language will demonstrate how the text uses language to avoid the appearance of mediation. In the chapter on Trump's battle with New York City over the rebuilding of the Wollman Ice Skating Rink, Trump recalls:

As I walked into the rink, I came upon a row of canvas sacks, abandoned and half covered by weeds. When I looked inside, I discovered that the sacks were filled with plants, which were once intended to be part of the new landscaping. Instead they'd been left on the ground, unopened, and had died. Just as I was making this discovery, a city worker walked by and stepped right on one of the few living plants on the site. He didn't look back. In a way, it was a perfect metaphor: the rink being trampled by one of the people who was being paid to fix it. (Trump *Art of the Deal* 208)

Even though this passage contains more description than much of *The Art of the Deal*, the images presented are simplistic. There are "canvas sacks" that are "filled with plants," but it is difficult to visualize these plant sacks because the passage provides no information about their appearance or their spatial orientation beyond the fact that they are "abandoned and half covered by weeds." It is unclear where the sacks are within the rink or how Trump "came upon" them. He finds them "as [he] walked into the rink," placing the sacks within the larger structure, but with no sense of relation to the rest of the environment. The language of the passage reduces the objects it describes to broad categories—plants, weeds, sacks, the ground. The narrative Trump provides for the plants is also disconnected from the bare fact of his observation. While he might be able to intuit that the plants "were once intended to be part of the new landscaping," the evidence he presents does not necessarily suggest that "they'd been left on the ground, unopened, and had died," due to neglect. It's equally plausible, for instance, that the plants may have been dead when they arrived or, perhaps, were not the correct plants. It is at this moment that the "perfect metaphor" suggests itself—"a city worker...[stepping] on one of the few living plants on the site." While the convenient timing of this worker's appearance certainly seems contrived, it is also notable that the "perfect metaphor" is not a metaphor at all when taken within the context of the passage. Throughout the Wollman Rink chapter, Trump contrasts New York City's allegedly incompetent and much-delayed treatment of the rink rebuilding with Trump's own alacrity, expertise, and civic-mindedness. In this passage, the City's incompetence is figured through synecdoche as the abandonment and destruction of the landscaping plants stands in for the larger inability to successfully rebuild the rink. The city worker stepping on the plant is not a metaphor—it does not make a comparison or bring in an outside image to illustrate Trump's point—the worker stepping on the plant is merely repetition, rendering in action what the passage has already illustrated through description.

Even in a moment of relative elevation, *The Art of the Deal* resists subtextual development, insisting instead that the surface meaning of Trump's experience and that of the text itself is the entirety of the text's meaning. *The Art of the Deal*'s anti-poetic approach to language implies a lack of mediation. By eschewing adjectives, images, and figurative language, the text produces an effect of immediacy, implying that the connotative and associative dimensions of language have peeled back in order to minimize the distance between Trump and the reader. Of course, this immediacy is itself artificial and even poetic in its own way, using the absence of figurative language as a kind of figuration. As *The Art of the Deal* was written by Tony Schwartz, purportedly with little direct input from Trump, the text must produce Trump's life while occluding the work of this construction. The text accomplishes this by embracing Trump's rhetorical tendencies while avoiding literary ornamentation. While *The Art of the Deal* emulates Trump's self-referentiality and his tendency to conflate his personal action with the actions of his firm, it eschews the syntactic and idiomatic idiosyncrasies of Trump's personal speech. In this way, *The Art of the Deal*'s prose style is premised on reproducibility. As with other aspects of Trump's signification, the style of *The Art of the Deal* can be easily reproduced by a range of writers and speakers within Trump's assemblage, creating a coherent sense of Trump's written voice. It does not matter that the voice of *The Art of the Deal* and Trump's subsequent autobiographies, *Surviving at the Top* and *The Art of the Comeback*, does not sound like Trump's spoken idiom. What matters is that the voice provides a vehicle for circulating Trump's life production. Similarly, *The Art of the Deal* provides the formal template for Trump's other autobiographies. For instance, like *The Art of the Deal*, *Surviving at the Top* is partially structured by deal narratives and *The Art of the Comeback* includes a time-stamped "day in the life" chapter that closely resembles a chapter in *The Art of the Deal*. Ultimately, the logic of the rink metaphor is the logic of the book's representational strategy, a collapse of figuration that insists that there's no distance or difference between thing represented and its representation. Thus, *The Art of the Deal*'s aesthetics embody the logic of corporate speech. When a corporation speaks, we understand that it is not the corporation speaking, but we treat it as though it is—just as the book is not actually Trump's speech, but we (like Trump himself) understand it as though it was.

## "It's in the Genes": Romantic Management

An important aspect of heroic management for Trump is that the heroic manager is a romantic figure, an individual whose will and subjectivity shape his environment and whose conceptual integrity is complete. Bradford and Cohen even go so far as to trace the figure of the heroic manager back to the American frontier in the early nineteenth century (Trump *Art of the Deal* 26). What's important for Trump is both the heroic manager's omnipresence and its opacity. As Mintzberg points out when dismissing the "Great Man School" of management, an analysis of the heroic manager as presented in CEO biographies and similar genres tells us little about actual management strategies (Trump *Art of the Deal* 11). Instead, some aspect of the heroic manager's functionality remains ineffable, inherent to the particular individual and irreducible to a principle. While this makes for bad management practice, as attested by over a half century's refutations, it produces an aura around the figure of the manager or CEO that allows the legitimization and translation of corporate power by figuring their success as a function of their particular personal qualities. While the life production of most CEOs manages the use of heroic management carefully as part of the negotiation of the metonymic relationship between CEO and firm, as we will see, Trump takes the cultural legibility of the heroic manager and intensifies the figure as part of his bid for legitimacy.

Popular management books also rely on the metonymic relationship between a CEO or manager and firm, positing that this relationship, if conducted correctly, can lead to greater success and productivity. At their core, management books offer theories and strategies for arranging and distributing power within an organization. For instance, *In Search of Excellence* by Tom Peters and Robert H. Waterman claims to distill observations from a range of successful companies into eight principles that might be enacted at any organization (Trump *Art of the Deal* 13). Another popular 1980s management book, *Managing for Excellence* by David L. Bradford and Allan R. Cohen, contends that American corporations are not realizing their potential because of outmoded leadership styles. Luckily, *Managing for Excellence* offers a model of "postheroic management" through a series of chapters that outline how to finesse one's management style to achieve "excellence" (Trump *Art of the Deal* 62). In both of these examples, the texts offer guidance on how to conduct oneself as a part of a greater whole and how to use one's position within a corporation to encourage others to more fully realize their metonymic potential as well. Crucially, in these instances, as in most management books, the advice comes from outside the corporation. Like the CEO in the CEO autobiography, the popular management book author positions themselves against, but distinct from the corporation itself, able to distinguish themselves in order to abstract and offer advice from experience. Part of what these texts offer is the possibility of doing the same. A manager who reads *Managing for Excellence* would begin to see their role as tethered to, but distinct from the firm, a part within the whole that holds a special significance to the ecosystem of corporate power in the organization. The text then offers the manager strategies for navigating this relationship and theories to legitimate these strategies. What is key in this reconceptualization is its portability that the role of the manager and the role of the corporation are abstracted to the point that the text can transmit relationship advice to as wide a segment of the corporate population as possible.

The second chapter of *The Art of the Deal* gestures towards the promise of the book's title in its formal resemblance to a chapter from a popular management book; ultimately, however, the chapter overwrites the reproducibility necessary to popular management theory with an image of Trump himself. Where most management books take a pseudo-social science approach, bolstering their claims with references to data and research, Trump builds an aesthetic, even romantic, orientation toward management in order to claim managerial authority without demonstrating it. The title of the chapter, "TRUMP CARDS: The Elements of the Deal," suggests a schematic breakdown of how to approach deal-making. One might assume that the chapter would provide a process or procedure by which to effect a deal, supplying one with "trump cards," or the winning gestures needed to succeed. Instead, these trump cards are cards that belong to Trump. At the outset, he declares that "deal-making is an ability you're born with. It's in the genes," and claims that "instincts" are more important than "being brilliant" (Trump *Art of the Deal* 32). In fact, Trump writes, "I can't promise you that by following the precepts I'm about to offer you'll become a millionaire overnight. Unfortunately, life rarely works that way, and most people who try to get rich quick end up going broke instead" (Trump *Art of the Deal* 33). Trump posits one's facility with the art of the deal as hinging on inborn traits, something unteachable, a kind of genius, harkening back to his initial statement in the text that deal-making is literally his art, like poetry or painting

(Trump *Art of the Deal* 3). He even doubts that "the precepts" he serves up will be of any use to anyone else because "life" resists an easy reduction to procedure. In this, Trump rejects the usual premise of the genre of management books—that organizational complexities can be approached systematically through attention to process and structure.

A short subtitle, encapsulating a precept sets off each of the "Trump Cards" presented in Chapter 2. What follows, however, is not a general application of the precept, but an illustration of how Trump performed a specific action under specific circumstances. While these illustrations are intended presumably to serve as examples, they lack either the generality or portability necessary to serve as a theory of management. For instance, Trump's first precept is "Think Big," which he introduces by declaring, "if you're going to be thinking anyway, you might as well think big. Most people think small…and that gives people like me a great advantage" (Trump *Art of the Deal* 33). To Trump, thinking "small" entails fear, as he claims that people "think small, because most people are afraid of success, afraid of making decisions, afraid of winning" (Trump *Art of the Deal* 33). Beyond this, however, "thinking big" is never defined clearly except that it is integral to "people like [Trump]." As is common throughout these examples, Trump becomes the ultimate expression of his precepts and the only way to fully embody his management strategy is to become more like him, to approximate his subject position. Trump provides the example that "It's nice to build a successful hotel. It's a lot better to build a hotel attached to a huge casino that can earn fifty times what you'd ever earn renting hotel rooms. You're talking a whole different order of magnitude" (Trump *Art of the Deal* 33). This example is connected to the initial precept of "thinking big" by the use of the second person pronoun that Trump had hitherto abandoned for the first person after his assertion that, "if you're going to be thinking anyway, you might as well think big." The hotel/casino example points to the way that "thinking big" seems to involve pursuing the largest and/or most expensive options one has available, but it also points to the irreproducibility of Trump's management strategy. If someone has the capital and wherewithal to build hotels, they are unlikely to be reading *The Art of the Deal* for advice. To the ordinary consumer, the addition of a "huge casino" to a hotel is an "order of magnitude," perhaps many magnitudes, beyond their capabilities. In fact, given the difficulty of obtaining the necessary permits, licenses, and properties to build a casino, a process Trump details at length in a later chapter, adding a casino to a hotel is something that is really only possible if one is Trump or very near to him, both in economic and social capital and in expertise.

This is in direct opposition to popular management books where the organizing principle of the genre most often involves moving from precept, to example, to application, premising replicability and portability. For instance, in *In Search of Excellence*, the title of each chapter reflects a supposed quality of a successful organization. In the introduction to Chapter 5, "A Bias for Action," Peters and Waterman begin by explaining that it is difficult to explain "action orientation, a bias for getting things done" (Peters and Waterman 119). They then move on to a specific example where they show "an executive…how it might be possible radically to simplify the forms, procedures, paperwork, and interlocking directorates of committees that had overrun his system," by taking the executive on a tour of another company (Peters and Waterman 119). The description of the tour occupies a paragraph, after which Peters and Waterman abstract the principle they are trying to explain. They first describe why "action bias" is important, and then describe how a lack of action bias negatively affects certain companies. Following this, they sketch the contrast between the mismanaged companies and the "excellent" companies (Peters and Waterman 120). Finally, they provide a sort of thesis statement, arguing that one can replicate the techniques that excellent companies use to promote action bias. The form here generalizes and promotes application. While the example mentions some minor specifics, the example describes them in broad terms as "task forces" and "committees," structures common to many organizations. The orientation here and in most popular management books is towards possibilities of identification, allowing the readers to see themselves in the text so they can replicate the processes and relationships the text advocates. In *Art of the Deal*, not only are the precepts opaque, their precise mechanisms or applications uncertain, the examples tend to premise replicability on irreproducible qualities. For instance, Trump writes, "one of the keys to thinking big is total focus. I think of it almost as a controlled neurosis, which is a quality I've noticed in many highly successful entrepreneurs," placing the "key" to this precept in attaining a pathology (Trump *Art of the Deal* 34). As with the "fear" attending "small thinking," Trump defines this neurosis negatively, writing, "where other people are paralyzed by neurosis, the people I'm talking about are actually helped by it" (Trump *Art of the Deal* 34). Trump thus suggests that in order to "think big" one must not only acquire a neurosis, but also have an unusual predisposition towards neuroses. As a result, it becomes impossible to enact the management philosophy Trump—it is an innate quality.

Trump's overwriting of the popular management genre rejects the generic tendency toward quasi-scientific trappings for a romantic orientation toward management that reduces management to its aesthetic, surface dimensions. For instance, under the heading "Know Your Market," Trump reiterates that the art of the deal is instinctual and inherent, writing, "Some people have a sense of the market and some people don't. Steven Spielberg has it. Lee Iacocca of Chrysler has it, and so does Judith Krantz in her way. Woody Allen has it...and so does Sylvester Stallone, at the other end of the spectrum" (Trump *Art of the Deal* 36). Therefore, while knowing one's market may be integral to success, in Trump's view, this sense is innate, unlearned. The company in which Trump places himself underscores his reduction of management to its aesthetic surface, listing only one "pure" businessperson, Iacocca, among film directors, a novelist, and an actor.[4] The list coheres because Trump does not distinguish between business and art, seeing both as acts of constructing the most appealing commodity for a given market. Out of all the auteurs on the list, however, Trump singles out Stallone as a direct point of comparison, writing,

> You've got to give him credit. I mean, here's a man who is just forty-one years old, and he's already created two of the all-time-great characters, Rocky and Rambo. To me he's a diamond-in-the-rough type a genius purely by instinct. He knows what the public wants and he delivers it. I like to think I have that instinct. (Trump *Art of the Deal* 36)

In his description of Stallone, Trump emphasizes Stallone's age, his characters, and that his genius is solely a product of his instincts, his "sense of the market." Stallone appeals to Trump as an image of genius and instinct because Trump sees himself in Stallone. Both Trump and Stallone are the same age, born only a month apart and the characters Stallone creates and plays are versions and extensions of himself. What Stallone markets is himself, just as Trump builds and trades on his own image. Unlike Krantz or Allen, Stallone's genius is "at the other end of the spectrum," unlimited in its appeal, "a genius purely by instinct." This is the specific instinct that Trump claims to have and that he places at the heart of his management "theory." It is an instinct for surfaces, an ability to sense how best to commodify an embodiment. Whether the embodiment is a character or a name on a building, the synonymous identification of the actor/manager and the character/product flattens management to a manipulation of outward signs rather than participation in a process.

By rejecting the reproducibility of his management philosophy, Trump figures himself as an intensification of the heroic manager. Like Stallone, Trump is the actor and the character, the producer and the product, collapsing the distinction between himself and his organization. Although the heroic manager is omnipresent in managerial discourse, it is not omnipresent within organizations. As Bradford and Cohen point out, most work can be completed "without heroics," though in moments of turmoil, "many managers instinctively revert to heroic images and action" (Bradford and Cohen 29). Trump enacts an intensification of the figure of the heroic manager by making himself ubiquitous in his organization, representing himself as the locus of all action and decision-making. In a discussion of a failed deal at Television City, Trump describes how, "I'd build NBC's headquarters myself...I'd also subsidize NBC's rent for thirty years...I'd be subsidizing NBC out of my own pocket," before explaining that,

> Ironically, there was almost total opposition to my offer within my own organization. Robert, Harvey Freeman, and Norman Levine felt that for me to agree to give NBC...subsidies before we knew what revenues we'd be earning was too great a risk. My feeling was that the risk was worth taking. (Trump *Art of the Deal* 232)

In this rare acknowledgment of the collective labor involved in the Trump Organization, Trump distinguishes himself slightly from his organization in order to reassert his complete control over it. The offer is "my offer" and the organization "my own organization," but the uncertainty is collective, "opposition...within my own organization" where a "we" faces risk. Trump then dismisses this uncertainty by a reassertion of his individual agency, predicated on his instincts, his "feeling" that determines the course of action. The uncovering of collective agency here serves only as a means for Trump to display his managerial style, to create a kind of crisis that a heroic managerial intervention can solve. As a result, there is no narrative tension from the disagreement; instead, the disagreement serves only to allow Trump to explain his reasoning for offering these incentives and to reinforce his control over the Trump

Organization. In this way, the gesture to collective decision-making actually reinforces Trump's collapse of the metonymic relationship between manager and firm as it demonstrates that collective input into decisions is beside the point.

## Structuring *The Art of the Deal*

Just as the typical CEO/firm relationship structures the average CEO autobiography, Trump's metastatic relationship with his firm similarly undermines and distorts the narrative structure of *The Art of the Deal*. Where most CEO autobiographies present a teleological narrative plotted to emphasize the distinctions between the CEO and the firm, *The Art of the Deal* is framed in a kind of continuous present that collapses distinctions between Trump and the Trump Organization as well as the past, present, and future. The text begins with a chapter written in the present tense purportedly describing Trump's work at the time of writing. This is followed by a chapter that purports to offer business advice, how to practice "the art of the deal." After this, the text begins an ostensibly chronological narrative, beginning with a chapter on Trump's childhood and family, before the bulk of the book begins a series of chapters, in chronological order, each dedicated to narrating a particular deal that Trump made. The text ends with a chapter that brings us back into the present with an eye toward the future. Across the text, however, there is a porousness that undercuts the text's chronology. As Trump speaks in the present, deals from the past surface as though they are still on-going, while discussions of the past frequently summon details and commentary from future events, transcending the moment being described. As a result, the text avoids a sense of progression, of growth, in the sense of development, and instead metastasizes the present Trump across time and space, embracing of growth as an increase in size, a kind of accumulation.

The text begins with a chapter titled, "Dealing: A Week in the Life," which purports to detail, day by day, Trump's engagement with a variety of projects, mostly real estate, and primarily by phone. Although the passage of time in the chapter is marked by time stamps and headings for each day of the week, every entry is written in the first person and present tense. As a result, the progression of the present only exists on the surface. Where other CEO autobiographies often describe the subject's work as part of the text's narrative, *The Art of the Deal* attempts to generate a sense of that work as a process, using the continuous present of the work week to create effects of simultaneity and saturation. Throughout the litany of phone calls Trump makes and takes are various mentions of many of the on-going projects the text covers in later chapters, such as the Wollman Skating Rink, the Trump Castle Casino, and the United States Football League (Trump *Art of the Deal* 15–17). While some of these mentions involve projects that Trump completed in close temporal proximity to the writing of the text, others were developed years in the past. As a result, each of these "deal narratives" is plugged into the text's continuous present, serving as a kind of annotation or gloss to Trump's executive temporality, adding depth to the initial chapter's breadth as the text progresses. Narratively, the discussions of the various deals the book covers serve to introduce Trump's various projects and provide a frame for understanding the rest of the text. At the same time, the simultaneity in which these various projects occur, sometimes out of time, flattens the narrative's teleology by removing the deals from their historical contexts and rejecting their narrative closure. Thus, the work of the Trump Organization at large, both historically and in the moment of the text, merges into the work of Trump himself. As we will see shortly, the avoidance of resolution enacted in this early chapter will ultimately factor into Trump's inability to produce the standard narrative of CEO autobiographies.

As a result, Trump enters the text as an action-focused manager, always engaged in work that never really ends. At the outset of the first chapter, Trump describes his unorthodox work habits, claiming, "Most people are surprised by the way I work. I play it very loose… You can't be imaginative or entrepreneurial if you've got too much structure. I prefer to come to work each day and just see what develops" (3). The continuous present of the "Week in the Life" serves to illustrate this claim, defining Trump's management style as improvisatory and intuitive, thereby granting Trump the kind of idiosyncrasy a heroic manager requires. This idiosyncrasy, however, goes beyond personality, and extends to Trump's method of working in its emphasis on imagination and fluidity, pointing back to his assertion that his work is a kind of art. This allows Trump to claim the position of heroic manager without actually demonstrating any facility for managing employees or workflow. In these instances, Trump manipulates the metonymic mechanisms of corporate speech, often opposing himself, figured as a first person pronoun against a corporate entity, as when he discusses a potential casino deal with Holiday Inn:

> When the board of Holiday Inns was considering whether to enter into a partnership with me in Atlantic City, they were

attracted to my site because they believed my construction was farther along than that of any other potential partner. In reality, I wasn't that far along, but I did everything I could, short of going to work at the site myself, to assure them that my casino was practically finished. (37–38)

Here, Trump and Holiday Inn are treated as equal entities, despite the opposition of singular and collective action. It is clear, however, that what Trump figures as the actions of himself as an individual are actually the result of collective effort. The "site," "construction," and "casino" belong to "him," but he has done no "work at the site," instead relying on employees to do the physical labor. In the end, though, to Trump, the real work of the deal is "confirming an impression they were already predisposed to believe" (38). This displaces the work of the Trump Organization onto Trump the heroic manager, not only aggregating the actual construction work to Trump's possession, but arguing that the only construction that mattered was the construction of an image for Holiday Inn to consume.

We might compare this moment to Iacocca's discussion of the congressional testimony he made in an effort to secure loan guarantees for Chrysler as it faced bankruptcy. In a chapter entitled, "Chrysler Goes to Congress," Iacocca describes his testimony in terms like, "Hour after hour I had to sit in the box and go on trial before Congress and the press for all of Chrysler's so-called sins of management—both real and imagined" (Iacocca 213). As with Trump and Holiday Inn, Iacocca distinguishes himself as an 'I' interacting with corporate, collective figures, "Congress" as well as "the press." The difference is that Iacocca carefully manages the relationship between his self-presentation as CEO and the firm. The title of the chapter folds Iacocca within the corporate entity of "Chrysler." The entire company does not go to Congress, just Iacocca and his aides, but he figures himself as a metonymic figure for the company he speaks for and as Chrysler. At the same time, he distinguishes himself as CEO at key points in order to highlight both his acumen and his affective experience. For instance, he writes,

> I was on my own in those hearings. I had to ad-lib everything. The questions came fast and furious and they were always loaded...I had to respond to everything off the cuff. It was murder. We were scolded for not having the foresight of the clever Japanese. (Iacocca 213)

While Iacocca speaks for and as Chrysler at these hearings, absorbing the criticisms directed at "us" for actions "we" did not take, he also emphasizes himself as a human individual who can be on "my own" and who has "to respond to everything." The effect is to carefully tether Iacocca to Chrysler in terms of responsibility—he has to justify the company's actions—while setting him apart as an individual who has his own affective responses to performing this duty. When Trump takes on Holiday Inn, the entire metonymic construction falls apart, folding all of the Trump Organization's actions and commitments into Trump's singular pronoun while also flattening any clear sense of Trump's individual experience as CEO. Even as Trump figures his actions as the actions of an individual, his affect is that of a corporate figure.

## The CEO Becomes

Development and progression are central narrative features of CEO autobiographies. The CEO/narrator learns, changes, and becomes alongside a dynamic, evolving organization. The development of the CEO enacts the CEO's maturation into the position of cultural and political authority that they assume at the narrative's culmination. In this emphasis on development and maturation, both of these corporate genres share formal similarities with the bildungsroman, what Bakhtin calls the novel of "becoming" or "emergence" (Bakhtin 20–21). For Bakhtin the crucial innovation of the bildungsroman is the development of a sense of the hero's growth in historical time, a dialogic development of the character and the world (Bakhtin 23). This resonates with Schoenberger's argument that CEO autobiographies "trace a trajectory in which the hero becomes his own, true self through passionate engagement with another. They are narratives of self-realization in which the realized or achieved self becomes a catalyst for change in the organization" (Schoenberger 283). In their melding of autobiographical and heroic narrative conventions, CEO autobiographies generally capture how the CEO's emergence dialogically alters the firm. The world of the corporation, always evolving in response to historical economic and political pressures, shapes the CEO even as the CEO intervenes in and shapes the development of the corporation.[5] The CEO's claim to cultural authority comes because of their ability to respond to historical forces over time. In *The Art of the Deal*, however, Trump does not change or develop as a character, but remains unchanged. The Trump that begins the text expertly managing a continuous present of phone calls is, in his contours, the same Trump who appears as a child alongside his father and who ends the text looking into a future of endless, ever larger deals. Just as Trump metastasizes his 'I' throughout the text, rewriting metonymic speech as personal speech and vice versa, Trump overwrites all historically contingent Trumps with the version of his life that signifies the Trump assemblage. What emerges over the course of the text is not Trump the hero, but the world, figured as New York City.

Beginning in the third chapter, where Trump briefly turns both autobiographical and retrospective, New York City serves as a site for development, growth, and change. The city begins as financially insolvent, poorly managed, and incompetent (Trump *Art of the Deal* 69). Over the course of the text, the city's prospects improve, often despite City Hall, as Trump's various deals get underway. Using his collapse of the CEO/firm dynamic to position himself as an opponent to the corrupt, bureaucratic, incompetent, and collective City, Trump depicts himself as a wellspring of New York City's renewal. The city, however, does not change in any fundamental or foundational way. Rather, it serves as a viable substitute for Trump's growth precisely because cities grow and change endlessly without drastically altering their basic character. Indeed, the particular kind of growth that Trump depicts, the consolidation or splitting of plots of land, the construction or destruction and reconstruction of structures primarily involves an endless overwriting through time of existing space. The city does not develop in the sense that it matures or grows wiser. Rather, mirroring Trump, it accumulates and grows bigger. Ultimately, the world that emerges over the course of *The Art of the Deal* is literally a world that increasingly belongs to and mirrors Donald Trump. Its own kind of metonymy governs the bildungsroman, CEO autobiography, or management book. A particular scene, event, or principle stands as an illustration of a period in a course of development, always suggesting while not containing the trajectory of the text's or character's development. At the end of these texts, one can look back and see how the different parts of the text relate to the production of the whole. In *The Art of the Deal*, the parts consume the whole and any slice of Trump's narrative contains the germ of the whole thing.

Trump's inability to emerge or to self-realize produces the text's inability to resolve or develop a standard narrative of becoming. As the eponymous head of a private company, Trump has no corporate ladder to climb, no internecine politics to navigate. The refusal of the metonymic relationship between manager and firm leaves Trump unable to emerge dialogically with historical time. As a result, even the most autobiographical moments of the text insist that Trump has always been a fully developed CEO. In the chapter, "Growing Up," Trump provides a brisk family history that primarily focuses on his father's business. When Trump discusses his own childhood, his main rhetorical move is to show that, even as a child, he embodied the same values and characteristics he claims in the text's present. For instance, Trump's first real discussion of his childhood begins with the statement, "I was drawn to business very early, and I was never intimidated by my father...we had a relationship that was almost businesslike" (Trump *Art of the Deal* 49). Here, business permeates Trump's character as both an interest and a means of conducting relationships. By describing his relationship with his father as "businesslike," Trump suggests that he was raised as a businessperson, already engaged in deals and negotiations from a young age, just as he is in the text's present. Similarly, Trump claims, "I was always something of a leader in my neighborhood. Much the way it is today, people either liked me a lot, or they didn't like me at all" (Trump *Art of the Deal* 49). In this instance, the narrative reaffirms Trump's life production in the present by locating in his childhood the same qualities he now wants to claim. Unlike the typical CEO, Trump does not realize what Schoenberger would call "his true self," but claims to have always been his true self (Schoenberger 285). Where other CEOs narrate their self-realization to invigorate their metonymic relationship to their firm, Trump, in constructing himself as a CEO, cannot produce himself outside of or against his eponymous company because there is no distinction, no dialogue between the two. Rather, like a corporate entity itself, Trump simply appears fully formed.

## Trumping Corporate Authority: Metastasis and Resolution

One of the uses of CEO autobiography is to translate cultural or economic authority into political power. Once the autobiography legitimizes the CEO as a member of the managerial elite, the text can either make the case for or serve as proof of the CEO's fitness to govern. Again, Lee Iacocca's *Iacocca: An Autobiography* serves as an archetype of this translation through its structure. Unlike *The Art of the Deal*, *Iacocca* follows a more typical autobiographical form, beginning in media res with Iacocca's banishment at Ford, before proceeding with a relatively chronological account of his life. However, the narrative does not conclude once Iacocca reaches events contemporaneous with the text's publication. Rather, the autobiographical narrative dissolves into a discussion of Iacocca's political prospects followed by a series of essays on various social, political, and economic issues, including a chapter titled, "Making America Great Again." While Iacocca denies any desire to run for president, he makes clear that he believes he could be president and that, underwritten by his corporate success, his political ideas are what he believes America needs.[6] The text thus enacts its translation of power. Rather than resolve or close the narrative, the CEO autobiography opens itself to the world—the CEO leaves off narration and begins to command.

The distorted metonymic relationship between Trump and the Trump Organization, however, precludes narrative closure at all points throughout *The Art of the Deal*. Each of the deal narratives within the text narrates a particular deal from its genesis to a kind of stasis. Where Iacocca's chapters function like chapters in a novel for much of the text, each chapter leading thematically and chronologically into the next, Trump's chapters are mostly discrete, opening on a scene that sets the stage for the next deal, but lacks a clear connection to what has immediately preceded it. In addition, each deal narrative is incomplete in some way—most of them end with some kind of futurity. For instance, the chapter on Trump Castle ends with a projection of revenues and the Wollman Rink chapter ends with Trump looking out his window "as he writes," at skaters on the rink (Trump *Art of the Deal* 164, 214). The ultimate resolution of these narratives is handled in the final chapter of the text where many of the projects mentioned in the first chapter are given headings accompanied by brief entries. The chapter fails to resolve many of the narratives effectively, however, instead either repeating information from the deal narrative itself, like the budget for the Wollman Rink project, providing only the barest information, for instance remarking that Trump enjoys spending time at Mar-a-Lago or that his apartment renovations were finished in 1987, or displacing resolution further into the future, as with the assertion about withdrawing his application for a Las Vegas gaming license that "I don't rule out building or buying in Nevada at some point in the future" (Trump *Art of the Deal* 239). This ambiguity is compounded by the final statement of the book, where, under the heading, "What's Next?", Trump admits, "I don't know the answer, because if I did, that would take half the fun out of it" (Trump *Art of the Deal* 242). Trump concludes the book by writing, "Don't get me wrong. I also plan to keep making deals, big deals, and right around the clock" (Trump *Art of the Deal* 243). Thus, the end of the book places itself outside and beyond the continuous present in which the text begins. Somehow, the present of the initial chapter is now in the past, and the narrative is in a new present oriented toward the future. What Trump promises is not future development, but more of the same, more deals and the pursuit of deals in a constant present, "around the clock," simultaneous and boundless.

Ultimately, *TRUMP: The Art of The Deal* is a simulation of popular corporate culture intended to produce a simulated CEO. Bloomberg is correct that Trump is a "pretend CEO," insofar as Bloomberg means that Trump does not have the same job responsibilities or obligations that a "real" CEO would have (Gstalter). In another sense, however, what Trump is exploiting is that the CEO in popular management culture is not a set of job responsibilities, but rather an image. Trump reduces the figure of the CEO to a series of surfaces and gestures that simulate constant action and consequential decision-making. Unlike other CEOs who use their autobiographies to render legible their actions and decisions against the history of their firm, Trump uses the genre for its genericity, how it structures the utterance to create the effects of action and consequential decision-making. An analogous figure appears in Trump's discussion of the deals he made to construct the Trump Plaza Hotel and Casino. After Trump put together the land parcels needed to build the casino, he describes how he sought a partnership with Holiday Inn to defray costs associated with building and running the casino. Before formalizing the deal, the board of directors of Holiday Inn wanted to visit the site to see how construction was going. Learning of this, Trump writes that he sprang into action, calling his foreman: "I said, I wanted him to transform my two acres of nearly vacant property into the most active construction site in the history of the world. What the bulldozers and dump trucks did wasn't important, I said, as long as they did a lot of it" (Trump *Art of the Deal* 142–143). Trump already has a "construction supervisor" on his payroll, indicating that he possesses the means to "[get] some actual work accomplished" if that was his goal. In this instance, though, Trump wants to produce an impression beyond ordinary construction work, emphasizing that the site must appear to be "the most active construction site in the history of the world." Trump insists here on the surface-level gesture that the appearance of great activity and action is more "important" than the utility of the action. The construction site stands in as an image of the work of *The Art of the Deal*. While the usual process of translating corporate power into the public sphere requires a CEO to live a life that they then produce as autobiography or a manager to live a life that they translate into a theory of management, Trump reverses the process. To be a CEO or a manager to Trump is to make the gestures of the executive managerial class, to produce a book that can circulate as proof of one's membership in that class. In this sense, the content of *The Art of the Deal* is not important, just as "what the bulldozers and dump trucks did wasn't important." Rather, it is *The Art of the Deal's* status as an object, a piece of popular corporate culture that can circulate widely, that benefits Trump's life production. Like the Holiday Inn board of directors, we saw the CEO autobiography or management book, and presumed that the person to whom it was attached was doing the work that such an object signified. He purports to produce a kind of text only produced by members of a particular social class and cachet, what Schoenberger calls "the executive managerial class," and thereby emerges as a member of that class. In doing so, Trump reveals the degree to which the constructs of popular management culture, like the CEO and the heroic manager, and popular management literature are fictions that naturalize neoliberal models of subjecthood while reifying inherently authoritarian corporate power structures.

## Notes

1 On Welch's autobiography, see: Bose, Purnima, "General Electric, Corporate Personhood, and the Emergence of the Professional Manager," *Cultural Critique and the Global Corporation*, eds. Purnima Bose and Laura E. Lyons. Indiana University Press, 2010: 28–63.
2 Mintzberg, 1973: Mintzberg assigns the image of the heroic manager to what he calls, "The Great Man School" of management (11). Mintzberg argues that these kinds of representations are useless for considering what managers do because they do not actually describe management, but rather personality.
3 Chia, Robert, "Reflections: In Praise of Silent Transformation—Allowing Change through 'Letting Happen'," *Journal of Change Management*, vol. 14, no. 1 (2014): 8–27; Ivanova, Olga and Sybille Persson, "Transition as a Ubiquitous and Continuous Process: Overcoming the Western View," *Journal of Change Management*, vol. 17, no. 1 (2017): 31–46.
4 Though Iacocca is included most likely not because of his success in business itself, but rather his success in circulating images of his success in business in order to translate that success into cultural and political power. After all, Iacocca's *Iacocca: An Autobiography*, a clear

model for Trump's life production, appears only three years prior to *Trump: The Art of the Deal*.

5 See, for instance, John Sculley's depiction of his negotiations with Bill Gates in 1985–1986 in *Odyssey*. The negotiations illustrate the degree of power and success Sculley had reached at Apple, but also depicts attempts to work in and against the historical forces shaping the computer industry in the mid-80s.

6 Iacocca ultimately refused to run, but the popular press pointed to his autobiography to support the argument that he should run in the popular press. See, for instance: Gailey, Phil, "Iacocca Disavows Effort to Draft Him as a Presidential Candidate," *The New York Times*, 18 Jul. 1986: A9.

## Works Cited

Bakhtin, Mikhail. "The Bildungsroman." *Speech Genres and Other Essays*, translated by Vern W. McGee, edited by Caryl Emerson and Michael Holquist. University of Texas Press, 2007, pp. 10–59.

Bose, Purnima. "General Electric, Corporate Personhood, and the Emergence of the Professional Manager." *Cultural Critique and the Global Corporation*, edited by Purnima Bose and Laura E. Lyons. Indiana University Press, 2010, pp. 28–63.

Bradford, David and Allan R. Cohen. *Managing for Excellence: The Guide to Developing High Performance in Contemporary Organizations*. John Wiley and Sons, 1984.

CBS News Investigative Unit. "Donald Trump Book Royalties to Charity? A Mixed Bag." *CBS News*, 11 Aug. 2016, cbsnews.com/news/donald-trump-book-royalties-to-charity-a-mixed-bag/.

Chia, Robert. "Reflections: In Praise of Silent Transformation—Allowing Change through 'Letting Happen'." *Journal of Change Management*, vol. 14, no. 1, 2014, pp. 8–27.

Gailey, Phil. "Iacocca Disavows Effort to Draft Him as a Presidential Candidate." *The New York Times*, 18 Jul. 1986, A9.

Gstalter, Morgan. "Bloomberg Calls Trump a 'Pretend CEO'." *The Hill*, 26 Jan. 2019, thehill.com/homenews/administration/427102-bloomberg-calls-trump-a-pretend-ceo.

Iacocca, Lee and William Novak. *Iacocca: An Autobiography*. Bantam, 1984.

Ivanova, Olga and Sybille Persson. "Transition as a Ubiquitous and Continuous Process: Overcoming the Western View." *Journal of Change Management*, vol. 17, no. 1, 2017, pp. 31–46.

Mayer, Jane. "Donald Trump's Ghostwriter Tells All." *The New Yorker*, 25 Jul. 2016, newyorker.com/magazine/2016/07/25/donald-trumps-ghostwriter-tells-all.

Mayer, Jane. "Donald Trump Threatens the Ghostwriter of 'The Art of the Deal'." *The New Yorker*, 21 Jun. 2016, newyorker.com/news/news-desk/donald-trump-threatens-the-ghostwriter-of-the-art-of-the-deal.

Mayr, Katharina and Jasmin Siri. "Management as a Symbolizing Construction? Re-Arranging the Understanding of Management." *Historical Social Research/Historische Sozialforschung*, vol. 36, no. 1, 2011, pp. 160–179.

Mintzberg, Henry. *The Nature of Managerial Work*. Harper & Row, 1973.

Peters, Thomas J. and Robert H. Waterman. *In Search of Excellence: Lessons from America's Best-Run Companies*. Warner Books, 1984.

Schoenberger, Erica. "Corporate Autobiographies: The Narrative Strategies of Corporate Strategists." *Journal of Economic Geography*, vol. 1, 2001, pp. 277–298.

Sculley, John and John A. Byrne. *Odyssey: Pepsi to Apple*. Harper & Row, 1987.

Stahl, Bernd Carsten. *Information Systems: Critical Perspectives*. Routledge, 2008.

Trump, Donald J. and Tony Schwartz. *TRUMP: Art of the Deal*. First Edition. Random House, 1987.

# 3   A Chevrolet in Tokyo

## Lee Iacocca, Japanese Management, and Donald Trump's *Surviving at the Top*

In a 1984 Chrysler television advertisement, CEO Lee Iacocca descends from darkness down a metal staircase. As he descends, he sadly states that many people do not believe America is great anymore. At Chrysler, however, they are doing their best. He then strolls through a simulated factory floor, passing technicians working on new Chrysler vehicles and pausing to identify the virtues of the cars. Finally, he stops behind a computer terminal and presses a button on a keyboard, and a graphic rendering of a sedan appears on the computer screen. Iacocca then explains, "Next year we will build a small car right here in America with quality that we're determined will beat the Japanese at their own game" ("1984 Lee Iacocca"). Marked as cutting edge through its connection with the computer terminal, the car symbolizes Chrysler's efforts to stave off Japanese economic competition, a key narrative element of popular corporate culture's advocacy for neoliberal reforms. Iacocca steps away from the terminal into an empty, black space. Echoing the 1980s popular corporate culture's insistence that America was losing its global supremacy to Japan, the ad tightens its frame around Iacocca's face, alone again, in darkness, as he says, "Quality, hard work, commitment. The stuff America was made of. Without them there is no future. I have one and only one ambition for Chrysler—to be the best. What else is there?" ("1984 Lee Iacocca"). The effect is ominous. "Quality, hard work, [and] commitment" are the qualities in which Iacocca claimed America has lost faith. Here, they are the very "stuff America was made of." While the commercial has its optimistic moments, celebrating sales of minivans and expressing "determination" to "beat the Japanese," the statement "without them there is no future" suggests a desperate battle for high stakes. Unless America recommits to the "stuff" of its making, "there is no future." The statement implies that Chrysler is not currently "the best," since this is an "ambition" of Iacocca's, something he wants to realize. Embracing neoliberalism's reduction of all interactions to competition, the commercial suggests that if Chrysler, and by extension America, cannot be "the best," then there is nothing else to be.

While Reagan used the slogan, "Make America Great Again," during his 1980 campaign, primarily on merchandise, the phrase was neither his only slogan nor a particularly major one (Dangremond). Similarly, when Bill Clinton used the phrase in his 1991 campaign announcement and again in a 2008 commercial supporting Hillary Clinton, "Make America Great Again" was not the primary or sole slogan of the campaigns (Dangremond). These instances illustrate the bromidic nature of "Make America Great Again," how it could be applied inoffensively by both conservative politicians running against progressive opponents and vice versa. For both Reagan and Clinton, "Make America Great Again" was just the sort of thing that a US politician says. The first presentation of "Make America Great Again" as shorthand for an ideological program occurs in Iacocca's 1984 *Autobiography*, the best-selling non-fiction hardback book of 1984 and 1985 (McDowell "Publishing" and "Iacocca"). In Iacocca's text, "Make America Great Again" is the title of an essay that lays out a populist, neoliberal vision for American economic and cultural revival. While Iacocca did not run for president, his *Autobiography* argues that he could have done so successfully and uses this argument to legitimate a series of essays that layout what a business-oriented, CEO-led US government might look like. As the leading CEO autobiography in the years leading up to Trump's *The Art of the Deal*, Iacocca's *Autobiography* provides generic markers that translate business authority into political authority, generic markers that underpin Trump's extended life production.

The 1984 Chrysler ad provides the basic schematic of the political positions Iacocca takes up in his *Autobiography* and thus undergirds Trump's ideological and aesthetic debt to Iacocca. In Iacocca's essays, "The Japanese Challenge," and "Making America Great Again," he expands the basic images of the ad into a geopolitical analysis and a policy program for restoring American greatness through subjugation of the state to corporate interests. Chrysler and Iacocca did not produce these ideas in a vacuum, however. Rather, like Trump, they leveraged cultural, economic, and political anxiety to make their case. Before turning to Iacocca's essays, it will be necessary to establish the historical and discursive context in which Iacocca rose to prominence. In particular, we must read the Chrysler ad, Iacocca's *Autobiography*, and Iacocca's presidential ambitions within the context of the popular corporate culture discourse surrounding (and constructing) the so-called trade war between America and Japan in the 1980s.

Lee Iacocca is an important antecedent to Trump in several ways, but scholars and the media have devoted little attention to the ways that Iacocca laid the grounds for Trump's life production and eventual political rise. In both his life production and his political involvement, Iacocca developed a kind of populist neoliberalism that Trump would imitate and eventually embody. A consideration of Iacocca's influence on Trump will illustrate the role that popular corporate culture played in developing the aesthetic and political ideals that Trump would exploit. Ultimately, I will demonstrate that Iacocca's life production provided both the structure and ideology that Trump would use to develop the autobiographical apparatus he would parlay into the presidency.

## "The Japanese Challenge"

The late 1970s was a time of global economic recession and change that proved particularly difficult for American corporations who faced for the first time since World War II global competition for American markets. As Erica Schoenberger describes, the mass production system that emerged after World War II was predicated on a continuous growth of productivity linked to advances in processes and technology (Schoenberger 44). By the 1970s, the system's ability to increase productivity began to fail at the same time that middle-class consumption of goods flagged. As these production techniques spread to the developing world, where a middle class had yet to emerge and there were fewer consumers for mass-produced goods, markets in Europe and America began to see an influx of cheap consumer products that offered American and European middle-class consumers significant choices for consumption, threatening American and European market share. In particular, Japan emerged as a competitive producer of automobiles and electronics. Japan used the techniques of mass production to produce a high quantity of goods, but, unlike manufacturers in America, developed systems to produce a greater variety of goods and to alter more quickly the styles and types of goods produced. According to Schoenberger, the range and flexibility of Japan's production techniques presented "the most far-reaching challenge to the existing system and the firms which were dominant within it" (Schoenberger 44–45).

The discourse of Japanese competition that emerges in management literature in the 1970s is part of the development of larger neoliberal formations. As Simon Springer argues, the economic recession of the 1970s led to "disillusionment" with government interventions in lives of people and corporations and an embrace of market forces as regulators (Springer 3). As neoliberalism took root in the United States and elsewhere, part of what Springer calls its "bureaucratic formation" involved deregulating business and transferring "public holdings over to the private sector of corporate interest" (Springer 25). Management writers, politicians, and CEOs used Japan's manufacturing success to argue for deregulation and an alignment of the state's interests with corporate interests. The nationalist flavor of the discourse and its anxiety about American prowess in the face of a foreign competitor produces emotional and patriotic arguments for accepting notions of organization that subjugate social, personal, and human interests to the pursuit of profit and growth. Part of the work of the management literature that disseminates the Japanese competition discourse, then, is to reorganize management structures at the corporate and state levels while legitimating the need and the urgency of this reorganization.

Circulating widely as *Iacocca: An Autobiography* sold over 2.5 million copies, Lee Iacocca's essays, "The Japanese Challenge" and "Making America Great Again," made a case to the American public for using the logic of the 1984 Chrysler commercial, itself an example of Japanese competition discourse, to drive US political and economic life. In his essay, "The Japanese Challenge," Iacocca outlines the main ideological points of Japanese competition discourse in contrast to Republican ideology as defined by Ronald Reagan. While he presents Reagan's neoliberal policies as a step in the correct direction, Iacocca argues that these policies are not adequately nationalistic. Iacocca argues,

> Japan's economic destiny was not left up to the free play of laissez-faire economics. Now, Japan is not Russia, which has a totally planned economy. Far from it. But Japan does have a system of goals and priorities that allows government and industry to work together to achieve their national objectives. (Iacocca 315)

To Iacocca, "the free play of laissez-faire economics" makes it possible for countries like Japan to outcompete the United States because the government allows markets to operate without intervention. As a result, Iacocca claims, US corporations are at a disadvantage because the governments of other countries protect their own markets and corporations. Iacocca "blame[s] the ideologues who seem to think that any government involvement in the national economy somehow undermines our free-market system" and advocates that the US government should intervene to protect American companies (Iacocca 322). In these passages, Iacocca promotes an idea common to popular management books of the 1980s that Japan's economic success was due in part to the Japanese government working to support Japanese corporations. Here, by figuring free trade conservatives as "ideologues," Iacocca borrows a common populist gesture, suggesting that free trade advocates in government are an elite group, unconcerned with the practical effects of their policies (Voelz 204). In doing so, Iacocca invites readers to shift their identification from political figures to corporate figures like himself, a move that prepares the grounds for Iacocca's argument that the United States needs to reorganize politically, socially, and economically to support corporate objectives.

In order to sell the reorganization of the United States to promote corporate interests, Japanese competition discourse emphasizes the severity and stakes of competition with Japan by insisting that America is no longer great. For his part, Iacocca figures this decline through a series of substitutions whereby the success of American business is coterminous with the US global authority. Iacocca argues, "we've lost some of our economic greatness" and asks, "how, in less than forty years, did we manage to dismantle the 'arsenal of democracy' and wind up with an economy that is flabby in so many critical areas?" (Iacocca 326). In fact, Iacocca casts the prosperity and expansion the United States experienced in the wake of World War II as the beginning of America's decline, arguing, "Our loss of leadership did not come overnight. The gradual erosion of our strength and power began in those halcyon years following World War II. But in no period of our history has America showed more vulnerability than in this past decade" (Iacocca 326). By invoking the phrase "the arsenal of democracy," Iacocca points to cultural conceptions that US industry is an extension or expression of the US political ideals. Iacocca uses this figure to shift the "loss" of "economic greatness" to a "loss of leadership" that results from an "erosion of our strength and power." What begins the passage as a loss of market share, an expression of the relative weakness of particular industries, ends with a nation in decline, no longer able to command respect or claim authority.

In decrying the US supposed decline, Iacocca echoes other management writers of the 1980s. Narratives of American decline are central to Japanese competition discourse because they provide both a rationale and a sense of urgency to calls for reforming American business practices. While Japan's economic success involved manufacturing and exporting goods to America, writers figure America's decline through a range of images that go beyond economic or industrial practices to the conditions of social, cultural, and political life. For instance, Ezra Vogel argued that the Japanese

> see America as a nation on the decline and Japan as a nation on the rise. Japanese visitors to the United States are no longer surprised by street crime and inner-city decay, by vandalized automobiles and trash-littered streets. They notice elaborate security measures and fear of strangers at night. (Vogel *Comeback* 15)

Here, the US loss of market share to international competition manifests as the loss of order and the threat of violence in the streets. The United States is "on the decline," "decay[ed]," covered in graffiti and garbage. In other instances, writers portray the decline in terms that are more abstract. For instance, W. Edwards Deming argued that American industry was in crisis and "only the transformation of the American style of management, and of governmental relationship with industry, can halt the decline and give American industry a chance to lead the world again" (Deming xiv). For Deming, it is not just that American industry is losing profits and market share, but that the US global standing as "leader" has diminished. In both cases, the US failure is a failure of management and the fate of corporate America intertwines inextricably with the health of the nation. By conflating the United States as a nation with the success of American corporations, these images invest neoliberal transfers of power and authority to corporations with a patriotic flavor. In order to restore America to its previous greatness, individuals need to embrace changes to their labor conditions and their consumption habits, even when these changes mean ceding power to management or selecting different products.

Iacocca's essay "The Japanese Challenge" immediately precedes "Making America Great Again," in his *Autobiography* in order to establish the urgency of the reforms for which the latter essay calls. In both essays, Iacocca produces images of a Japanese invasion of US territory to underscore the economic threat. Again, connecting economics to US political values, Iacocca exclaims, "Question: what do you call a country that exports raw materials and imports finished goods? Answer: a colony. Now, is *that* the kind of relationship we want to have with Japan?" (Iacocca 320). By conflating sovereignty with economics, Iacocca suggests that Japan could usurp the US independence. The specter of colonial status poses a threat to deep-seated cultural notions of personal independence while suggesting subjugation and exploitation. The military language that Iacocca uses underscores this threat. For instance, he argues, "They've already taken electronics. They've taken sporting goods. They've taken copiers. They've taken cameras. They've taken a quarter of the automobile industry," describing Japan's increased market share in certain economic sectors as though they are conquered territories (Iacocca 320). Continuing his critique of "free trade," Iacocca laments that "we're sitting by and watching Japan systematically capture our industrial and technological base," and remarks, "Japan appears capable of looting our markets with impunity" (Iacocca 326). While the image of America as a colony suggested subjugation, these descriptions of Japan "taking," "capturing," and "looting" make the threat apparent. In Iacocca's formulation, America's territories are economic, they are "our markets," "our industrial and technological base." By invoking the corporate first person plural, Iacocca collapses the distance between nation and economy and between individual and corporation. As a result, to defend the United States from imminent "invasion," true patriots must stand ready to support economic reforms that support American corporations and penalize foreign companies.

In these images of invasion, Iacocca draws on common images in Japanese competition discourse, usually embodied by the preference of consumers for Japanese products. For instance, in Kenneth Blanchard and Spencer Johnson's *The One Minute Manager*, the character of the senior manager illustrates a point about quality by asking the aspiring manager, "Do you see how many foreign cars there are on the road?" at which "The young man looked out at the real world and said, 'I see more of them every day. And I guess that's because they're more economical and they last longer.'" The senior manager then stands "at the window lost in his thoughts. He could remember, not so long ago, when his country provided the technology that helped to rebuild Europe and Asia. It still amazed him, that America had fallen so far behind in productivity" (Blanchard and Johnson 20–21). It is important that the young manager look out at "the real world," implying both the world outside of the corporate workplace and the world outside of the book's fable-like narrative. In the "real" world, "foreign cars" fill the road and increase in number "every day," ceding American space to foreign goods. When the senior manager looks out the window, he sees concrete evidence of America's "fall." The United States has become so weak and unproductive that the countries the US "rebuilt" now supply the US with "technology."

In other instances, writers presented the presence of foreign products and investment in the United States in more violent terms. H. Edward Wrapp, for instance, decried business schools teaching outmoded theories of management, claiming "the business schools have done more to insure the success of the Japanese and West German invasion of America than any one thing I can think of" (qtd. in Peters and Waterman 25). As in *The One Minute Manager*, Wrapp raises the specter of World War II, only here, Japan and West Germany are "invading" a United States weakened by poor management practices. Similarly, summing up American reluctance to change, Vogel, in his *Japan as #1*, explains that "to expect Americans, who are accustomed to thinking of their nation as number one, to acknowledge that in many areas its supremacy has been lost to an Asian nation and to learn from that nation is to ask a good deal" (Vogel *Japan* 225). In perhaps the most histrionic vein, Clyde V. Prestowitz writes, "In 1986 alone, $6 billion of Japanese money went to U.S. real estate, including the Exxon, the ABC, and the Tiffany buildings in Manhattan. By 1987, it was estimated that nearly half the office space in downtown Los Angeles was in Japanese hands" (Prestowitz 307). Here, Japan is literally buying up the United States, both in terms of culturally prominent buildings and in terms of raw space. Given this rate of progression, we must infer that in the near future, Japan just might own everything in the United States. It is then, Prestowitz suggests, that we might "become a kind of fourth-world country," in which case he wonders, echoing Iacocca, "what are the hazards of becoming a colonial territory again?" (Prestowitz 305).

In the management literature of the 1970s and 1980s, Japan is on the cusp of defeating America, creating a cultural crisis in which American national identity and sovereignty is supposedly in question. With each of these images, however, the writers seek not to record a real threat, but to create the effects of one. While Japan's market share increased over the 1970s and 1980s, Japan's gains were not the zero-sum game that management writers made them out to be. By the mid-1980s, the trade war between the two countries shifted to different terrain, focusing less on Japanese exports and more on US access to Japanese markets. While there were upheavals in certain industries, like the automotive industry, and shifts in markets, the United States was not in danger of becoming, as Iacocca says, a "colony" of Japan. Rather, the threat of a foreign invasion that would destabilize life in the United States provided cover for U.S. corporations to pursue deregulation, union-busting, automation, and a bald focus on profits for shareholders over all else. After trumpeting the danger of American decline and foreign invasion, the management literature that participates in the Japanese competition discourse makes broad recommendations for the reordering of American society to better allow corporations to grow and profit while normalizing corporate conceptions of power and authority.

Japanese competition discourse participates in the production of what Wendy Brown, developing a term of Foucault's, calls neoliberalism's "political rationality" (Brown 121). Brown describes political rationalities as "world-changing, hegemonic orders of normative reason, generative of subjects, markets, states, law, jurisprudence, and their relations" (Brown 121). The changes in manufacturing, marketing, organization, and economy advocated by the producers of Japanese competition discourse represented a dramatic alteration of American business practices, labor conditions, and cultural conceptions. While scholars have written much about the practices themselves, their effectiveness and applicability, scholars largely have not considered Japanese competition as a discursive phenomenon, shaping subjects and producing new social and political relations.[1] The threat of economic domination by the Japanese produced the grounds for CEOs like Iacocca to seize cultural capital and claim a right to govern. As Brown notes, part of neoliberalism's ascendance intertwined the terms "governing" and "managing," "index[ing] an important fusion of political and business practices" (Brown 123). By yoking nationalist sentiment—that the United States is under attack and in decline—to business concerns and thereby collapsing distinctions between business and politics, Japanese competition discourse positions CEOs and businesspeople as qualified political actors.

What little critical attention Iacocca's *Autobiography* has received treats the text as the prototype of the contemporary CEO autobiography, an exercise in business celebrity.[2] While this is true, the text is also fundamentally political, in both its engagement with electoral politics and its expression of neoliberal ideology. Crucially,

Iacocca extended his life production across subsequent books and media appearances through a series of political feints, threatening to run for president of the United States while denying any ambition to do so. This strategy allowed Iacocca to generate considerable economic capital through books sales while garnering cultural capital as the US public validated Iacocca's claims to political authority. In order to sustain this life production, Iacocca must offer a political position that is distinct from those of the Republican and Democratic parties, tantalizing readers with an option outside of the binaries of the US political system. As we will see, the political ideas that Iacocca espouses are neither radical nor particularly well fleshed out. Instead, Iacocca's political positioning inheres in his construction of himself as a heroic manager guided by principles of what Brown calls "governance" (Brown 131). Unlike the typical politicians of the Democratic and Republican parties, Iacocca suggests that businesspeople like himself are unhampered by the compromises, traditions, and inefficiencies of politics. Instead, Iacocca dangles in front of readers the image of decisive, action-oriented, pragmatic presidential leadership driven by business principles imported into government from Iacocca's experience as an automotive executive. This image, of course, ignores the actual operations of the US political system, a fact that renders the image both impossible and alluring.

### *"We've Got to Face Reality": MAGA as Virtual Politics*

It is not clear that Lee Iacocca ever actually intended to run for president. Even as he makes gestures in 1984's *Iacocca: An Autobiography* and 1988's *Lee Iacocca's Talking Straight* that promote the idea that he could run, win, and govern, Iacocca denies any desire to do so. Rather, releasing his autobiographies in presidential election years and winking at efforts to draft him as a candidate, Iacocca seems to have preferred to revel in the cultural capital and book sales that feinting at a presidential run afforded him. As we will see in the next chapter, Donald Trump would eventually borrow this strategy from Iacocca. The penultimate essay in his *Autobiography*, "Making America Great Again," brings the full rhetorical weight of Iacocca's engagement with the CEO autobiography and political essay genres to bear on carving out a conceptual space in American politics for the businessperson presidential candidate. "Making America Great Again" converts Japanese competition discourse into a political platform driven by the logic of the 1984

Chrysler commercial. Most of the policy positions Iacocca outlines reiterate the concerns raised in any number of the 1980s management books preoccupied with using the threat of Japan to remake US society. More important is the essay's work as a performance of Iacocca-as-president, a move that recasts America's challenges as issues of management. In staging this performance, Iacocca generates the prototype of the businessperson candidate, a heroic manager outside of and even against the US binary politics who can right America's ship of state. However, while Iacocca uses critiques of Democrats and Republicans to position the businessperson candidate as apolitical, he actually endorses a conception of executive power that is inherently authoritarian and anti-democratic, rooted as it is in corporate hierarchies and ideas of authority.

The political prescriptions laid out in Iacocca's "Making America Great Again" are familiar. In the essay, Iacocca describes a set of policy positions and ideas that translate the populist neoliberalism that infuses the book into a political platform. From competition with Japan and skepticism of pure free trade, to the revitalization of manufacturing and restoring a sense of lost "greatness," the program Iacocca outlines resembles Trump's in contour and in many particulars. It is the 1984 Chrysler commercial transmuted into governmental policy. In the essay, Iacocca argues that the United States has lost its greatness because it does not have a coherent "industrial policy." To Iacocca's mind, the state must do more to support national business against foreign competitors in order to revitalize the US economy. Iacocca proposes a six-point plan to "form the basis for a new industrial policy" that includes pursuing "energy independence," "[limiting] Japan's market share for certain critical industries," "[facing] reality on the costs and funding mechanisms for federal entitlement programs," providing "special education grants and loans...for high-technology fields of study," offering "new incentives to increase research and development efforts in the private sector," and "[establishing] a long-term program for rebuilding America's arteries of commerce," by which he means infrastructure (Iacocca 332–333). In addition, Iacocca laments the national debt, decries high interest rates, and suggests the establishment of a "Critical Industries Commission" in which "government, labor, and management could get together" and "recommend specific measures to strengthen our vital industries" (Iacocca 333).

These proposals, however, do not constitute enactable policy, but rather create an image of policy intended to validate Iacocca's presidential fantasies. What Iacocca presents instead is a simulation of policy designed to distinguish him from Democrats and Republicans without opening himself up to critique. For instance, this is the entirety of the third point of Iacocca's "six-point program":

> As a nation, we've got to face reality on the costs and funding mechanisms for federal entitlement programs...The answer has always been right in front of our noses: we can't continue to pay out more than we take in, and that will mean some very painful adjustments. (Iacocca 332)

Here, Iacocca does not specify which "federal entitlement programs" need reform, nor does he specify what "fac[ing] reality on the costs and funding mechanisms" of these programs would entail. He could be talking about food stamps, subsidized housing, or Medicaid, but he could also be referring to Medicare or even Social Security. It is also possible he means all of these things, even though changes to certain programs might draw more or less objection politically. It is also unclear what the "very painful adjustments" would entail. They could take the form of cuts to or the elimination of programs in order to reduce what we "pay out," but the "adjustments" could also be something like tax increases that raise how much "we take in." Rather than cool down the "hot potato" by offering a vision of how to address the issue, Iacocca doubles down on its indeterminacy. At its core, the point is simply a chestnut of neoliberal common sense—do not spend more than you can afford. Without any specificity or vision, the sole purpose of including social programs in Iacocca's policy platform is to make it clear that Iacocca is not a Democrat, just as his critiques of free trade make it clear that he is not a Republican. Like the social program point, the substance of most of Iacocca's policy proposals is not detailed and none acknowledges the realities of politics. For instance, none of the policies acknowledges how it would pass through the legislature, nor do any of the policies acknowledge the complexities of the US foreign relations, even as the policies propose radical alterations in relationships with OPEC and Japan. Rather, the point of the policy platform is simply to resemble a policy platform and thereby provide Iacocca's pretend candidacy with an aura of legitimacy. Just as Iacocca would not actually run for president and thus risk losing, he avoids articulating detailed policy proposals that could be criticized or rejected. This enables Iacocca to generate investment in his candidacy—his ideas seem pragmatic, "common sense"—without assuming any personal risk.

Rather, the purpose of "Making America Great Again," both as a text and as a politics, is to collapse the distance between images of the heroic manager and the president in order to generate cultural and political capital for the CEO. In Iacocca's case, "Making America Great Again" provides him with space to perform being president. Iacocca begins the essay by recounting a time that he used an op-ed piece to make a presidential gesture. This opening salvo illustrates the translation of Iacocca's corporate authority into the political sphere while constructing an image of Iacocca as a businessperson president. Iacocca recalls how, "In the summer of 1982, I wrote a piece for Newsweek where I proposed a simple way of cutting the national deficit in half," asking, if shared sacrifice could save Chrysler, "Why couldn't the principle of 'equality of sacrifice' be applied to the federal deficit as well?" (Iacocca 324). Iacocca imagines himself as president, writing, "My plan was simple. First I would cut 5 percent a year out of the defense budget... Then we'd call in the Democrats and say to them" that they need to cut social programs to the same degree (Iacocca 324). Across these sentences, Iacocca moves from corporate policy to political policy, from speaking as a CEO to speaking as though he were president of the United States, demonstrating the fluidity with which he views the translation of corporate to political power. Indeed, even the public staging of the editorial is a political intervention founded in corporate ideology. The translation of power is underwritten by Iacocca's claim that, prior to publishing the editorial, he "went to every CEO I knew on Wall Street and asked them: 'What would happen if the President went on TV and announced that he was cutting the federal deficit in half?'" (Iacocca 325). According to Iacocca, "They all agreed that this announcement would trigger the biggest investment binge in our history. It would restore our credibility as a country. It would prove that we knew what we were doing" (Iacocca 325). The circumstances surrounding Iacocca's editorial both enact and reduce the democratic mechanisms of US politics. Iacocca runs a kind of campaign, pitching his idea to "every CEO I knew on Wall Street," developing a consensus about his proposed policies before producing them as the editorial. However, the only people consulted are executives and the only result that matters is economic. Iacocca circumscribes both who has input into the decision and how to measure the decision's effect.

In addition, Iacocca's plan is merely a succession of mediated images, revealing the degree to which Iacocca conceives of the president performing the symbolic work of the heroic manager.

The president would go "on TV and [announce]" the reduction of the debt. The "investment binge" would happen not because of the reduction of the debt, but rather because of the "announcement" itself. Iacocca calls for cuts of $15 billion from the defense budget and $15 billion from "social programs," and the generation of revenue from a $15 billion "surtax on imported oil" and a $15 billion gas tax (Iacocca 324–325). Iacocca does not describe or acknowledge the political complexities of achieving this plan. Indeed, the only image of implementation is the image of President Iacocca "calling in the Democrats" and telling them to cut the social safety net. In Iacocca's formulation, the president of the United States can simply order things into law. This sense is supported earlier in the text when Iacocca discusses his incredulity that Loan Board chairperson Don Regan refused to honor Chrysler's requests to buy back suddenly valuable loan warrants from the federal government despite Iacocca's request that then President Reagan intervenes. Iacocca writes, "Even now, I can't believe it. Where I come from, if I as a CEO tell someone to do something and I never get an answer back, I fire him. It's incredible that this guy Regan could sit out this guy Reagan" (Iacocca 284). Iacocca cannot believe that his discussion with the president did not result in an immediate change of affairs because, to Iacocca, an executive officer should have complete and total authority.

These images are seductive, forming the core of Making America Great Again as a virtual politics. Iacocca's solutions sound reasonable and equitable—he even specifies that this "shared sacrifice" will be spread across the two political parties and both employers and employees. The logic of Iacocca's proposed actions follows the logic under which most Americans live their lives, as well, in that most people exist in relationship to some sort of boss or authority who can make unilateral decisions. For people who feel unrepresented by traditional politicians, the image of the businessperson candidate that Iacocca constructs has populist appeal. The "I" of Iacocca's *Autobiography* appears unmediated, speaking directly to his readers from a position outside of, but qualified to speak on, politics. Conceiving of the president as a heroic manager whose actions take immediate effect seems in this regard to be an intensification of political representation; the desires of the people directly transmitted from the people represented through the representative without the diluting effects of deliberation and compromise. In this sense, the president as heroic manager serves the same symbolic function as management in general, standing as a symbol of the nation's decision-making process (Mayr and Siri 172). However, the heroic manager is an effect of the need to represent the diffuse and untraceable actions of the firm, a way of consolidating complex processes into a legible figure. It does not function as a mode of governance within the firm. In fact, many management texts position their theories of leadership against the image of the heroic manager, arguing that unilateral, top-down management does not foster productivity and growth (Mayr and Siri 165). Viewing the president of the United States as a heroic manager encourages an authoritarian vision of the presidency in which the various checks and balances of the US governmental system dissolve in the face of the president's will. Thankfully, as with his policy platform, Iacocca did not intend to enact his vision of the presidency. Rather, he uses this image of the president as heroic manager to distinguish himself from elite politicians who make a career out of negotiations and compromises.

## Surviving at the Top

Trump's second autobiography, the 1990's *Surviving at the Top*, emulates the structure of Iacocca's *Autobiography*, concluding with a section entitled, "On Toughness," in which Trump outlines political positions and floats the idea of running for president. Trump published *Surviving at the Top* in a moment of crisis, facing deep debt, failed business prospects, and having endured a public and messy divorce from Ivana Trump. The book's publication two months ahead of schedule would have provided Trump with an influx of cash, although ultimately, despite seven weeks on the *New York Times Bestseller List*, the book's sales were disappointing (Cohen). As with Trump's successive political books, Trump's flirtation with presidential politics in *Surviving at the Top* is less about a sincere interest in higher office and more about the way that political ambitions might sell more books. Just as Trump used the moves of CEO autobiographies in *The Art of the Deal* to construct himself as a member of the executive managerial class, the move towards politics in *Surviving at the Top* reinforces Trump's claim to executive status while attempting to drive interest in Trump as a cultural figure. The politics that Trump outlines in *Surviving at the Top* draws on and intensifies the populist neoliberalism that Iacocca espoused, feeding Japanese competition discourse through the lens of Trumpian aesthetics to produce the foundation of the political gestures Trump would eventually use to win the White House.

The politics that Trump outlines in the final section of *Surviving at the Top*, titled "On Toughness," involves outward demonstrations of power and authority by the figure of a heroic manager, embodied here by Trump himself. He begins with himself, declaring, "I have a reputation for being tough, and I'd like to think it's justified," before going on to define toughness as "a quality made up of equal parts of strength, intelligence, and self-respect" that can "involve some old-fashioned ass-kicking," but which "has nothing to do with bullying people" (Trump 207–208). By drawing this distinction, Trump suggests that toughness is about directing one's power and authority toward accomplishing one's external objectives. The reaction of those over whom someone exercises power does not matter. Instead, one should use one's power for one's own gain. The example Trump gives is an extended anecdote in which he matches wits with the director of the Foundling Hospital in New York, a nun named Sister Cecilia (Trump 209). The Hospital sits on a desirable piece of land in New York City, and Trump approaches Sister Cecilia about selling it, but the Sister rejects his offer. Trump decides that he needs a personal connection to Sister Cecilia and the Hospital in order to make the deal (Trump 211). After arranging an introduction through a friend's sister, a nun herself, and using his Catholic connections, Sister Cecilia agrees to sell Trump the site (Trump 213).

On the surface, the Foundling Hospital deal is structurally and tonally similar to Trump's other deal narratives. However, the context of the narrative changes its resonance. Following Trump's explanation of toughness and preceding Trump's pivot to American politics, the Foundling Hospital deal enacts the translation of business acumen into politics. Initially, Trump claims that the anecdote illustrates how he "especially admire[s] toughness in the people I'm negotiating with" (Trump 209). Instead, the anecdote really illustrates how Trump's business experience allows him outmaneuver his opponents. In the story, Sister Cecilia is not triumphant. There is no difference described between the substance of Trump's initial offer and the offer Sister Cecilia finally accepts. Instead, Trump gets what he wants by accessing the power of his business network. His friend's sister, Sister Irene, operates a Catholic television station in New York and has connections to the Hospital (Trump 212). In addition, Trump brings to his second meeting with Sister Cecilia a friend of his who sits on the hospital board (Trump 213). Sister Cecilia bases her resistance in principle—Sister Irene tells Trump Cecilia is doing what is best for the hospital (Trump 212). Despite this, Trump wins out because his only principle is toughness itself, a concept he associates with sports and competition. Trump ends the anecdote with real estate rivals clamoring to make offers on the site, only to become enraged when discovering that the deal had already closed (Trump 213). Unlike many of Trump's deal narratives, the Foundling Hospital narrative emphasizes Trump's reliance on other people to complete a deal. In doing so, the narrative argues for the political efficacy of Trump's business strategies. The relationships he has forged through other deals allow him to exert the pressure necessary to perform successfully the idea of toughness that he has described. The narrative implies that the other real estate developers are either unable to leverage their networks to secure the deal or else unwilling to operate outside of the strict confines of the system at hand. They wait for the Diocese to advertise the sale of the Hospital in a brochure before calling, a hesitation that causes them to lose out. By recasting a typical Trumpian deal narrative in a political context, Trump uses his autobiographical apparatus to produce his life as latently political. Without making substantive changes to his brand or even his literary style, Trump retroactively invests his life production with political potential.

*Surviving at the Top* activates this potential by offering Trump's first foray into political life production. Immediately following the Foundling Hospital narrative, Trump pivots to national politics, opposing his notion of toughness to one of "weakness." Where the Hospital narrative illustrates Trump's ability to convert business toughness to political toughness, Trump turns to draw on a range of tropes from Japanese competition discourse to argue for America's decline while demonstrating what his vision of toughness would look like on a global scale. Trump argues that if the United States "fail[s] to address the challenges that are before us on the international business and economic scene, America's role as the leading nation in the free world will be in serious jeopardy in the next ten or fifteen years" (Trump 213). As in other popular corporate cultural artifacts of the long 1980s, Japan's ascendance is a sign of America's decline. Trump rails against the automotive trade imbalance, the size and proliferation of Japanese banks, and the inability of US politicians to demonstrate "toughness" in the face of Japanese competition (Trump 216–217). Trump's solution to this supposed decline is, of course, to be tough, but in his descriptions of his reforms, it is clear that the kind of toughness Trump is espousing requires embracing a corporate and authoritarian orientation toward governance.

Like Iacocca, Trump takes a dim view of politicians, casting them, in a populist move, as an elite group that cannot accomplish the work necessary to reverse the US decline because of their dependence on electoral politics. The contrast Trump draws between politicians and businesspeople, however, is more abstract than Iacocca's rendering, an effect of Trump's toughness/weakness dichotomy as well as his embrace of neoliberalism's gender politics. The problem, according to Trump, is that "politicians" "by nature…are weak or worried about offending some special interest… as a result, they deal exclusively in compromises and limp concessions" (Trump 216). According to this account, the very "nature" of politicians is problematic. They are always subservient to others, "weak or worried," qualities that contrast with the "toughness" and confidence of Trump's embodiment of the heroic manager, a figure that, in his construction, works to advance only itself. That Trump describes politicians as dealing "exclusively in compromises and limp concessions" suggests that politicians operate by sacrificing some degree of their own objectives, a position at odds with Trump's insistence that deal-making is a zero-sum game. As the Foundling Hospital narrative illustrates, a Trumpian politics does not require concessions or compromises, but rather an intensification of one's own position. Trump reinforces this notion by writing, "a person may be able to survive in politics or a State Department job with no discernible talent, but in business—whether you're a man or a woman—you must have…'balls'" (Trump 218). Trump singles out the United States State Department because it is the seat of US diplomacy. Not only does diplomacy require the kinds of compromises and concessions at which Trump sneers, these compromises and concessions are at the heart of the US "weakness," according to Trump. As with his phrase "limp concessions," Trump connects business acumen to masculinity, suggesting that only the machismo and bravado of a businessperson is adequate to the task of restoring the US global standing.

Trump's central argument draws on the tropes of popular corporate culture that concretize the US loss of global market share in images of violence and crime. For Trump, the issue is ideological: "The United States has a great system of government and a beautiful philosophy…Our problem is that we've stood behind our ideals only sporadically in recent years" (Trump 213–214). According to Trump, positive examples of "standing behind our ideals" include Reagan's handling of the 1982 air traffic controllers' union strike, the US invasion of Grenada, the capture and extradition of

Manuel Noriega and Reagan's airstrikes against Muammar Gaddafi (Trump 214). The national ideals embodied in these examples pro-corporate union busting, defending national interests through violence, and using violence to discipline other countries and individuals. In each of these instances, a person, group, or nation contested the will of the United States and lost, just as Trump's will subdued Sister Cecilia. Similarly, Trump recounts the reaction to the newspaper ad he took out in 1989 condemning as guilty the Central Park Five. Trump's ad serves as a harbinger of his later law and order rhetoric, proclaiming in capital letters, "BRING BACK THE DEATH PENALTY. BRING BACK OUR POLICE!" (Waxman). Trump recounts that once the ad was published, "I got calls from seven or eight top politicians, congratulating me for taking a stand and saying they agreed" (Trump 225). When pressed as to why these "prominent people...with much power and influence to get things changed," would not "take a similar position publically," Trump claims the politicians replied, "I'd like to, Donald, but it's such a controversial issue. When you're in politics, it's touchy. You can't really come down hard on things like this anymore" (Trump 225). Again, politicians appear weak and ineffectual in contrast to businessperson Trump, whose ad cried, "What has happened to the respect for authority?" and declared, "CIVIL LIBERTIES END WHEN AN ATTACK ON OUR SAFETY BEGINS!" By drawing this contrast, Trump argues that even on social and cultural issues, businesspeople are more effective than are politicians at accomplishing objectives. Unwilling to "take a stand" or demonstrate "toughness," politicians are helpless to solve social issues, in Trump's accounting. In both instances here, Trump associates good governance with public displays of authority and power, whether in the form of bombs or polemic newspaper ads. What matters is not the justness of the action or its concordance with Constitutional precedent or ideological principle, but rather the appearance of authority as embodied in the surety of the action, the confidence with which it is performed, and the decisiveness of its effect.

Trump dramatizes this notion of authority in order to demonstrate his potential fitness for dealing with the US competition with Japan. Trump relates how a friend of his asks Trump to take a meeting with a businessperson described as one of Japan's wealthiest people (Trump 219). Trump reluctantly agrees, but claims to forget about the meeting until the day of. A photographer enters Trump's office without knocking, taking pictures as an entourage of subordinates, "each one looking like a high-powered businessman in his own right," enter the room, followed finally by their boss (Trump 220). Trump describes, "My wealthy Japanese visitor didn't even say good morning to me; he just started speaking. 'I want real estate,' he stated. 'What?' I asked. 'I want real estate for investment purpose'" (Trump 220). Trump indicates his displeasure to his friend, who is also in the room, and then says to the businessman, "The relationship between your country and mine has changed greatly in our lifetimes, hasn't it?" to which the man replies, "Japan used to be down here...and America was up here. Now, Japan is up here and America is way down there. We no longer admire your country the way we used to. But I came to talk about real estate for investment purpose" (Trump 220–221). Trump then throws the man and his entourage out of his office, remarking, "I didn't have any qualms about showing them...the door because the wealthy Japanese gentleman was...extremely rude. I only wish that I could say he was wrong" (Trump 221). In this vignette, Trump takes care to paint each Japanese visitor as a "high-powered businessman," emphasizing a sense of entitlement by noting that the men entered his office without knocking and that the wealthy businessman offered no greeting or nicety. In a nod to Japanese competition discourse, the Japanese businessman is seeking to buy US real estate in order to make money, raising the specter of an America owned by foreign interests. However, the Japanese investors are on Trump's turf, in his office, and he uses his authority both as a businessperson, signified by his office, and as a politically "tough" figure, to throw the Japanese out of an American space, denying them the opportunity to purchase American property. In doing so, Trump demonstrates characteristics of the neoliberal populism that Iacocca espoused. In the narrative, written for US audiences, the reader is supposed to identify with Donald Trump based on national pride. Despite class differences and Trump's overweening self-importance, he becomes a figure of a strength and decisiveness that symbolizes an America run by tough businesspeople who can reject foreign economic intrusion and restore America's pride.

Trump's plan for America's revitalization institutionalizes the symbolic logic of Trump's narrative about the Japanese businessperson, offering an intensification of Iacocca's plan for "Making America Great Again." In his *Autobiography*, Iacocca suggests the creation of "a Critical Industries Commission—a forum where government, labor, and management could get together to find a way out of the mess we're in" (Iacocca 333). The purpose of this commission would be to "recommend specific measures to strengthen our vital industries and to restore and enhance their competitiveness in international markets" (Iacocca 333). Central to Iacocca's plan is his notion of shared sacrifice. Before the government would intervene to save a failing corporation, management and labor would both have to agree to concessions (Iacocca 333). The description of Iacocca's plan emphasizes the equality of the different actors, a "tripartite coalition," but subjugates the needs and priorities of each group to a conflation of national and corporate interests. For instance, while management might need to agree to "plow back [the corporation's] earnings into job-creating investments—in *this* country," labor, figured as "the unions," might need "to agree to restraints on the runaway medical costs that are now built into our system," meaning restrictions on the use of employer-supplied health insurance (Iacocca 333–334). The government would intervene to bailout the corporation once the company meets these conditions. Typical for Japanese competition discourse, Iacocca's plan views the state's role in economics as one that protects a nation's corporations and provides resources to advance their interests in the understanding that corporate interests and national interests are the same. At another point, Iacocca suggests, "I'd like to see a system where we brought in twenty top managers to run the business side of the country and maybe even paid them $1 million a year, tax-free…we'd see a lot more talented people interested in public life" (Iacocca 275). Here, Iacocca sets the foundations for Trump's proposals in *Surviving at the Top* by reiterating popular corporate culture's insistence that only managers and businesspeople are suited for controlling the nation's economy while underscoring the populist claim that "talent" cannot be found in traditional politicians and bureaucrats.

Similar to Iacocca, Trump conflates national and corporate interests while arguing for state support for US corporations. However, Trump intensifies Iacocca's proposal by suggesting that the state legitimates a complete managerial takeover of the US economy and trade. Trump calls for the formation of "a kind of all-star panel that would oversee America's negotiations with Japan, Europe, and other areas needing special attention" (Trump 222–223). The members of the panel would be "corporate leaders, independent dealmakers, and other nonpolitical public figures," who would be "vested with as much authority as our Constitution would permit" (Trump 222–223). Trump argues that his proposed panel could solve America's economic issues and restore the nation's reputation abroad "in a matter of months" (Trump 222–223).

In Trump's vision, the US Constitution serves as a cover to transfer economic and political authority to a small group of wealthy CEOs and financiers who, given "a free rein," will restore America's greatness in a short period of time, a feat politicians supposedly had tried to accomplish and failed. Where Iacocca's plan modifies for the national level his shared sacrifice strategy for running a corporation in crisis, a move that suggests that the state should be run like a corporation, Trump simply advocates putting CEOs in charge of the economy with as little accountability and regulation as possible. He provides a list of figures he says would be good candidates for the panel, including Jack Welch, Henry Kravis, Ron Perelman, Ted Turner, and Carl Icahn (Trump 222–223). The list names ten white men: four media executives, three financiers, and three CEOs. Taken in aggregate, the imagined panel is composed of men who, like Purnima Bose's description of Jack Welch, represent the "ghoulish" face of capitalism (Bose 51). In fact, the list notes Kravis is "the country's leading practitioner of leveraged buyouts" that "Bob or Sid Bass" are "investors *extraordinaires*," and Perelman is "another LBO wizard" (Trump 223). Their participation in the financialization of the US economy and increasingly elaborate practices of corporate raiding are the qualities that make these people prime candidates for the panel. In other words, their vampiric nature is their selling point. Importantly, Trump would repeatedly float Kravis for a cabinet position during Trump's 2016 campaign and Icahn would serve as an "informal advisor" until media coverage of his trading activity forced him out (DiChristopher and Everett). By appointing figures like Steve Mnuchin, Rex Tillerson, Linda McMahon, Wilbur Ross, and Louis DeJoy, Trump enacted, in part, the scheme laid out in *Surviving at the Top*, turning cabinet and executive branch positions involved in economics and international relations over to CEOs who then performed their duties like CEOs. While this produced consternation among critics and ambivalence among Republicans, this sympathy between *Surviving at the Top* and Trump's political actions demonstrates that even Trump's governance is more about life production than statecraft—he lived out the book that was written in his name.

The function of the list within the text, however, is not only to imply an attitude toward governance, but also to produce Trump as a CEO who could govern. Each of the people on the imagined panel stands as a heroic manager and successful embodiment of an individual who models their life on that of the firm. Trump lists Welch, Eisner, and Icahn next to the names of General Electric, Disney, and

TWA, respectively. Closely tethered to the corporations they manage or the financial processes they have mastered, each name on the list represents an individual instance of corporate success, neither fully human nor fully firm. At the same time, the list's emphasis on financiers, media tycoons, and celebrity CEOs reveals the degree to which Trump associates business success with the appearance of business success, whether it is exchanging byzantine financial instruments and stock options increasingly disconnected from physical reality or overseeing the production of images and cable news programs that construct reality for their viewers. While Trump is, of course, neither the kind of investor nor the kind of CEO that the list valorizes, he constructs himself as the kind of public figure that each of these CEOs cuts. Trump emphasizes this similarity by immediately adding himself to the list, writing, "If I were selected to serve on this council…I'd propose: the imposition of a 20 percent tax on imports from Japan, Germany, and other countries that don't play by the rules" (Trump 223). By suggesting that he would be a credible candidate for the panel he imagines, Trump associates himself with the other men on the list, using the appearance of similarity between these figures and himself to suggest that he possesses the same business and financial acumen that they do.

In doing so, Trump allows another important slippage, suggesting tariffs on Japanese and German imports as well as those of "other countries that don't play by the rules" (Trump 223). As a real estate developer and autobiography producer, Trump's knowledge of imports is undoubtedly limited. Trump might have experience with certain construction materials, like steel, but the scope of his business limits whatever knowledge he possesses. Similarly, the people on the imagined panel would have only tangential or limited knowledge of Japanese and German imports, since many of them are media executives and financiers or CEOs in highly specific industries. The practical knowledge that Trump or any of his doppelgangers might have, however, is unimportant. The production of these figures as businesspeople for public consumption necessitates a flattening of economic specificities and industry-specific knowledge, a flattening that these kinds of figures encourage because it increases their cultural and political power. Acting as a heroic manager, Trump first "proposes" the imposition of the "20 percent tax," but then imagines,

> So what if the Japanese slapped a tax on us in response…Even as I write this, I can hear the howls of protest from the foreign businessmen who'd be affected—and can see them pounding

on the doors of senators and congressmen, demanding to be heard. But I wouldn't feel pressured by those tactics, as the politicians involved no doubt would. Rather, I would take that strong reaction as an indication that I'd done the right thing. And then I'd move on to the next case. (Trump 223–224)

Trump moves into the present tense to emphasize his personal action, "even as I write this," before implying that "foreign businessmen" have a relationship with "senators and congressmen," after all, they are close enough to access "the doors" of Congress and "the politicians involved" would "feel pressured" by them. At this point, Trump has separated himself from the panel. He is no longer "proposing" an idea to the panel, but imagining his own unilateral enactment of that idea and its effects. Neither the reaction of the "foreign businessmen" nor "the politicians" matters or has any bearing on the proceedings. Trump instead decides he has "done the right thing" and "move[s] on to the next case," emphasizing his decisiveness, his imperviousness to political pressure, and his ability to get things done.

As an action, the imposition of a 20% tariff on imports from any number of countries lacks any specificity or justification. That Trump follows his imagined tariff imposition with the claim that "America has been weak...in dealing with other nations" suggests that the primary objective of the tariffs would be a show of force, to give the appearance of the "toughness" that Trump espouses (Trump 224). As in the narrative where Trump threw the Japanese businessman out of his office, this policy proposal serves primarily to underscore Trump's insistence that a heroic manager is what America needs to reverse its decline. The specification of a 20% tariff, the list of countries, beginning with Japan, the boogeyman of popular management discourse, each of these features serves not to produce a viable or actionable plan for economic growth, but rather to give the appearance of one. Unlike Iacocca or Perot, both of whom would construct "Making America Great Again" platforms out of Japanese competition discourse, Trump rightly assumes that detailed policy proposals are less rhetorically effective than gestures of executive authority. Trump repeats this gesture by following his corporate panel proposal with a self-congratulatory discussion of the controversy surrounding the ad he took out about the Central Park Five, a moment discussed above. Like the imaginary tariff imposition, the all-caps law and order ad offers little in the way of specific policy or ideological reasoning. Instead, it is another gesture of executive authority, a public demonstration of interventional action, this time in the social sphere, predicated on the assumption that the executive managerial class has a right to speak authoritatively on public and political matters.

Like Iacocca, Trump attaches demonstrations of his ability to wield executive authority and his solutions to America's supposed problems to a coy denial of electoral ambitions. The goal for both men is not to support an actual presidential run, but to create buzz around the possibility of their running for office. In doing so, they are able to influence public perceptions about the suitability of corporate leaders as presidential candidates without having to assume the risks of actually running. For Iacocca, this allows him to influence policy, while Trump most likely hoped the buzz would sell books. After describing the supposedly positive reactions to his Central Park Five ad, Trump writes,

> Whenever I've taken a stand like that in public, people ask me if I have any plans to run for elective office. The answer is no. I'm not a politician. I wouldn't want to get involved in the compromises, the glad-handing, and all the other demeaning things you have to do to get votes. Most of the best people we've had in government lately have, I've noticed, been appointed to their posts. (Trump 226)

Here, Trump directly echoes Iacocca who writes,

> while I might enjoy being President, it's strictly a fantasy because I couldn't imagine running for office. These guys are programmed like robots sixteen hours a day—lunches, dinners, the banquet circuit, shaking hands, going to the gates of the factories—it's endless. (Iacocca 275)

In addition, another of Iacocca's quips when questioned about his presidential ambitions was to claim that he would only serve if appointed, rather than elected. In both instances, Trump and Iacocca reject traditional political gestures that require them to produce their lives in deference to the citizenry. The US democratic rituals, like campaigning, hosting fundraisers, forming coalitions with special interest groups and other constituencies, are antithetical to images of the heroic manager. To Trump it is "demeaning" to have to seek votes, while Iacocca argues that he has already made these gestures, arguing that he has given enough speeches and glad-handed enough already (Iacocca 275). These sentiments reflect the authoritarian conceptions of power inherent to corporate culture. The heroic manager does not defer or consult. His only concerns are efficiency and profit. His only constituency the shareholders. While on the surface these gestures may not seem politically savvy, implying as they do a lack of concern or understanding of democratic norms, they serve as a populist repudiation of the political elite whose pressed blue jeans and state fair photo ops ring hollow to many Americans.

In this way, an authoritarian posture reads as refreshing, a kind of businesslike authenticity, while also allowing both Trump and Iacocca to claim that they are not suited to politics. Iacocca claims he is "too outspoken" and "too impatient" to be president (Iacocca 275). Trump writes that he would

> have to face one big obstacle if I ever did make a serious run for public office: Americans have become so accustomed to professional politicians that when they are faced with a strong personality—a man or woman of action—they are afraid, or at least very wary. (Trump 226)

Trump goes on to suggest, however, "when we fear leaders of great passion...what we often forget is that the other side fears them too," before recounting how Hitler admired Winston Churchill (Trump 226). Trump implies that Americans who would not vote for him embody the very characteristics that the chapter derides—fear, weakness, inaction. Trump drives home his production of himself as a "strong personality—a man...of action," who is a "leader of great passion," by reducing World War II to a contest between two heroic managers, individual personalities given over to action and upon whom everything rests (Trump 226). In doing so, Trump suggests that he has all of the qualities needed to make America great again while implying that his possession of those qualities is precisely why he may never be elected to office. Trump thus leaves himself as a tantalizing, but unobtainable solution to America's problems. The circulation of this argument that America needs a strong, outspoken leader unconcerned with party politics and democratic norms paves the way for the reality of Trump's presidency, even though the discourse primarily seeks to sell books.

## Notes

1 See, for instance: Stewart, Paul, *Beyond Japanese Management: The End of Modern Times?*. Frank Cass, 1996.
2 On Iacocca, see: Dionisopoulos, George N., "A Case Study in Print Media and Heroic Myth: Lee Iacocca 1978–1985," *The Southern Speech Communication Journal*, vol. 53, no. 3 (1988): 227–243 and Thorpe, Judie Mosier, "Lee Iacocca and the Generation of Myth in the Spokesman

Advertising Campaign for Chrysler from 1980–1984," *Journal of American Culture*, vol. 11, no. 2 (1988): 41–45. On Business celebrity, see: Guthey, Eric, Timothy Clark, and Brad Jackson, *Demystifying Business Celebrity*. Routledge, 2009.

## Works Cited

"1984 Lee Iacocca Chrysler Commercial." *YouTube*, uploaded by runfromcheney09, 23 Nov. 2008, https://www.youtube.com/watch?v=nppKMomMP-4.

Blanchard, Kenneth and Spencer Johnson. *The One Minute Manager*. Harper Collins, 1982.

Bose, Purnima. "General Electric, Corporate Personhood, and the Emergence of the Professional Manager." *Cultural Critique and the Global Corporation*, edited by Purnima Bose and Laura Lyons. Indiana University Press, 2010, pp. 28–63.

Brown, Wendy. *Undoing the Demos: Neoliberalism's Stealth Revolution*. MIT University Press, 2015.

Cohen, Roger. "Sales of Trump's Book Are Lagging." *New York Times*, 10 Nov. 1990.

Dangremond, Sam. ""Who Was the First Politician to Use 'Make America Great Again' Anyway?" *Town and Country*, 14 Nov. 2008.

Deming, William E. *Out of the Crisis*. Massachusetts Institute of Technology, 1986.

DiChristopher, Tom and Everett Rosenfeld. "Carl Icahn Resigned from Trump Advisor Role Ahead of Article Alleging Conflict of Interest." *CNBC*, 20 Aug. 2017, www.cnbc.com/2017/08/20/carl-icahn-resigned-from-trump-advisor-role-ahead-of-article-alleging-conflict-of-interest.html.

Dionisopoulos, George N. "A Case Study in Print Media and Heroic Myth: Lee Iacocca 1978–1985." *The Southern Speech Communication Journal*, vol. 53, no. 3, 1988, pp. 227–243.

Guthey, Eric, Timothy Clark, and Brad Jackson. *Demystifying Business Celebrity*. Routledge, 2009.

Iacocca, Lee and William Novak. *Iacocca: An Autobiography*. Bantam, 1984.

Mayr, Katharina and Jasmin Siri. "Management as a Symbolizing Construction? Re-Arranging the Understanding of Management." *Historical Social Research*, vol. 36, no. 1, 2011, pp. 160–179.

McDowell, Edwin. "'Iacocca' and 'Wobegon' Top-Selling Books of '85." *The New York Times*, 6 Jan. 1986.

McDowell, Edwin. "Publishing: 'Iacocca' Reaches Millionth Copy." *The New York Times*, 14 Dec. 1984.

Peters, Thomas J. and Robert H. Waterman. *In Search of Excellence: Lessons from America's Best-Run Companies*. Harper & Row, 1982.

Prestowitz, Clyde V. *Trading Places: How We Are Giving Our Future to Japan & How to Reclaim It*. Basic Books, 1989.

Schoenberger, Erica. *The Cultural Crisis of the Firm*. Wiley, 1997.

Springer, Simon. *The Discourse of Neoliberalism: An Anatomy of a Powerful Idea*. Rowman & Littlefield, 2016.

Stewart, Paul. *Beyond Japanese Management*. Frank Cass, 1996.

Thorpe, Judie M. "Lee Iacocca and the Generation of Myth in the Spokesman Advertising Campaign for Chrysler from 1980–1984." *Journal of American Culture*, vol. 11, no. 2, 1988, pp. 41–45.

Trump, Donald and Charles Leerhsen. *Surviving at the Top*. Random House, 1990.

Voelz, Johannes. "Towards an Aesthetics of Populism, Part I: The Populist Space of Appearance." *Yearbook of Research in English and American Literature (REAL)*, vol. 34, 2018, pp. 203–228.

Vogel, Ezra F. *Comeback, Case by Case: Building the Resurgence of American Business*. Simon and Schuster, 1985.

Vogel, Ezra F. *Japan as Number One: Lessons for America*. Harper Torch Books, 1979.

Waxman, Olivia. "President Trump Played a Key Role in the Central Park Five Case. Here's the Real History behind *When They See Us*." *Time*, 31 May 2019.

## 4 The President Makes All the Difference
### Genre, Image, and Becoming a Business Candidate

Over the course of Donald Trump's career, he has released a steady stream of mass-market books, all of which participate in the production of his life. *TRUMP: The Art of the Deal* gave way to *TRUMP: Surviving at the Top*, *TRUMP: The Art of the Comeback*, and *TRUMP: How to Get Rich*, an autobiographical quartet yoked together through their titles, their material aesthetics, and their formal contours. Like *The Art of the Deal*, each of these books draws on a conflation of the CEO autobiography and popular management guide genres to produce a public image of Trump as a businessperson. In 2000, however, Trump revealed his debt to the aesthetic and political practices of Lee Iacocca and Ross Perot by releasing a text entitled *The America We Deserve* as part of a bid for the presidential nomination of Perot's Reform Party. Where Trump's autobiographies, beginning with *Surviving at the Top*, would nod to politics, floating the possibility of a presidential bid as a means of generating book sales, *The America We Deserve* is a campaign policy book, an understudied genre of text that combines the ostensibly unmediated first person voice of life writing with arguments for political programs. While Trump would release another autobiography after this (*How to Get Rich*) as well as other minor works, the campaign policy book would become an increasingly important genre for his life production as he released texts in the run up to the 2012 and 2016 elections.

Popular corporate culture has infected the life production of political candidates in the United States, shaping how they represent themselves as well as how these representations circulate. The political campaign has always been a kind of life production, narrating a candidate's life to fit the public's expectations of candidacy. However, as neoliberal subjects, twenty-first-century US political candidates operate under the logic of corporate personhood, using multimedia assemblages to construct political brands and market candidacies.[1] Campaign autobiographies and policy books play an important role in these assemblages. Campaign books are corporate in the collective sense, composed by multiple people and operating alongside social media, advertisements, public appearances, and images to produce the candidate. However, these books are increasingly corporate, too, in how they signify. As with the reversal from autobiography to life production, the campaign autobiography or policy book has often become more important than the candidacy it supposedly supports. The books allow candidates to circulate and generate financial and political capital, producing investments in the candidate's causes, even if the candidate has no hope or even intention of winning. For instance, Herman Cain received criticism in 2011 for seeming to use his political campaign to sell his campaign autobiography rather than using the book to sell his politics (MacNicol). Similarly, Tim Ryan's presidential campaign gained little traction or interest, but coincided with the release of *Healing America*, a rebranded edition of an earlier book by Ryan. This development in campaign literature mimics the legitimizing effects of the CEO autobiography, signaling in the book's raw existence that the candidate has a right to pursue political power.

One might object that the campaign autobiography is not a corporate genre. After all, campaign autobiographies have played a role in US politics since the birth of the Republic and corporations themselves do not run for office. As Sidonie Smith has shown, however, the campaign autobiography is capacious, drawing on an array of genres to produce its narratives (Smith 526–527). Over time, campaign autobiographies have changed, increasing in number, but also in their debt to neoliberal genres like the self-help guide and management book. For instance, where Ryan's *Healing America* advocates "mindfulness" as a solution to America's woes (Francisco e35), Gillibrand's *Off the Sidelines* "recycles [the] entrepreneurial feminism" of Sheryl Sandberg's *Lean In* as Wendy Raphael Roberts points out (e18).[2] In both cases, popular corporate and neoliberal discourses enhance the marketability of the books and the candidates, suggesting that these discourses have eclipsed the purely political in terms of legibility. In addition, as Smith argues, the contemporary campaign autobiography is a corporate production, the product of a collaboration between numerous writers, advisors, marketers, and publishers (Smith 526). As a result, campaign autobiographies have become corporate, adopting both corporate discourses and corporate practices to legitimate their presence in the market.

Pundits and scholars alike dubbed Donald Trump's 2016 primary and election victories as surprises, reflecting a sense of incredulity at Hillary Clinton's loss, but also at the repugnant, extreme Trump's appeal to voters. Throughout the 2016 election season, indeed, well into his term in office, the news media dubbed Trump a "political neophyte," denigrating Trump's abilities while reinforcing a key pillar of his political brand—that he was not a politician (Cassidy). However, an examination of Trump's life production reveals that his victories were not surprising precisely because he was not a political neophyte. By the time Trump won the 2016 election, he had spent nearly twenty-five years floating the idea of his candidacy in his books, a strategy he borrowed from Lee Iacocca in order to generate economic and cultural capital. Not coincidentally, that quarter century also saw the development of cultural expectations for the postmodern business candidate, an image rooted in Iacocca's feints and embodied first by Ross Perot in 1992 and 1996. As a result, the viability of a businessperson with little or no experience in political office as a candidate for president of the United States developed significant populist appeal. As we will see, Trump's well-established life production regime as well as his ability to fulfill generic expectations of how a business candidate should appear positioned him for success. This is not to say, of course, that Trump won the election on purpose. Rather, this chapter will examine how Trump's political books draw on the representational strategies of campaign literature to play the political futures market, accidentally leading to a successful candidacy. Ultimately, I will argue that Trump succeeded where other business candidates failed because, where other candidates attempted to fit their lives into presidential expectations, Trump used his life production to construct an image of the presidency that fit his life.

## Campaign Books and Political Futures

As Stephanie Li and Gordon Hunter point out, US presidential candidacy now comes with the expectation that the candidate has a published book on offer (Li and Hunter 420). This expectation emerges as campaign norms have changed over time. As Richard J. Ellis and Mark Dedrick argue, the presidential candidate as active campaigner did not become the expectation until Franklin Delano Roosevelt, as presidential candidates realized that there was rhetorical power in bringing themselves into proximity with potential voters (Ellis and Dedrick). Towards the end of Ronald Reagan's time in office, Craig Fehrman argues, the publishing industry underwent changes that made the production of "blockbuster" presidential books an economically attractive venture (Fehrman 469). The advent of the internet and digital campaign strategies in the twenty-first century allows candidates new opportunities to produce their candidacies for public consumption. Sarah Banet-Weiser argues that the branding of political campaigns becomes increasingly important to candidates after Barack Obama's 2008 victory rested largely on Obama's successful promulgation of his brand across digital platforms (Banet-Weiser 126). An important dimension of Obama's campaign brand was the publication of 1996's *Dreams of My Father* and 2006's *The Audacity of Hope*, memoirs that Li points to as a turning point in the production of these kinds of texts (Li e50). Just as Iacocca feinted at higher office to increase the economic and cultural capital generated by his *Autobiography*, US politicians have begun to turn to life production as a means of generating their own capital.

The proliferation of campaign autobiographies and campaign policy books in the last two decades points to the increasingly financialized logic of the US political marketplace.[3] Where the campaign autobiography once operated strictly as a kind of promotional material, circulating alongside the other elements of a political campaign to bring the candidate into proximity with readers, in the past twenty years, the genre has detached itself both from the campaign and from the contents of the text itself. Instead, candidates produce texts that bet on future campaign cycles and media topologies, seeking to generate cultural, financial, and political capital, even if (perhaps, especially if) the candidate does not make a successful run. For instance, Representative Tim Ryan's 2018 *Healing America* is a reissue of Ryan's 2012 *Mindful Nation*.[4] By publishing *Mindful Nation* in 2012, a presidential election year, Ryan capitalized on the increased interest in politics and the concomitant increase in the value of having a political book in the marketplace to raise his visibility, generating cultural capital. In its 2012 context, *Mindful Nation*, with its sedate, blue and red cover, threads the line between inspirational and political text, using its political association to sell its brand of mindfulness. However, when *Healing America* appears in 2018, now with Ryan's youthful smiling face on the cover, it takes on new significance, serving as a campaign book for Ryan's abortive presidential campaign. Here, the mindfulness becomes a kind of politics. The text itself was generated as a kind of speculative investment, putting cultural capital into the political marketplace in the hopes of profiting off the election cycle as well as the national mood.

Potential candidates compose these texts to capitalize on shifting political markets, building in strategic ambiguities of genre and image to allow for readings that generate capital under different circumstances. For instance, Kirsten Gillibrand's 2014 *Off the Sidelines* takes its title from the name of Gillibrand's super PAC, founded in 2011 to support women running for office. As Roberts notes, Gillibrand's text, with an introduction by Hillary Clinton, first functioned to support Clinton's 2016 campaign before becoming Gillibrand's "de facto campaign memoir" when Gillibrand ran in 2020 (Roberts e18). The image of Gillibrand as a neoliberal feminist thus strings together the text's shifts in genre as it moves from a political memoir that raises Gillibrand's national profile and establishes her political brand in 2014, to an auxiliary campaign text for Clinton in 2016, to a campaign autobiography in support of Gillibrand's own campaign in 2020. The presence of Gillibrand's book in the cultural marketplace produces a constellation of relationships as time passes and the political market shifts. When Gillibrand ran for president herself, she developed a campaign brand that ideologically and aesthetically emerges from *Off the Sidelines'* market fortunes. Gillibrand presented herself as a feminist candidate, highlighting the influence of her mother and grandmother on her politics, a major theme in *Off the Sidelines*.[5] The legibility of this political brand relies on the cultural capital Gillibrand produced over the previous six years through the circulation of her book, allowing Gillibrand to campaign, for instance, as a kind of successor to Hillary Clinton without having to mention Clinton directly. While it is unlikely that many people actually read Gillibrand's memoir, the text provides a ground for these other representations, supplying images, themes, and narratives that can be taken up in television ads, social media campaigns, and interviews. Thus, the role of the campaign memoir in establishing brand potentialities is crucial. The book serves as a reservoir of images the candidate's assemblage can develop, deploy, suppress, or manipulate based on the fluctuations of the political marketplace.

The news media in the United States plays an important role in the rise and fall of any given presidential contender. Seeking to generate economic capital through advertising and cultural capital by fulfilling brand expectations or by offering a premium experience like a debate or an accurate poll, media corporations produce narratives about political candidates that influence citizens' perceptions of the election, the viability of candidates, and the state of the electoral process. In particular, a candidate's "electability" and ability to manage the image of their campaign receives disproportionate coverage. A report on the 2016 election by Harvard's Shorenstein Center on Media, Politics, and Public Policy, for instance, reveals that 56% of media coverage of the 2016 primaries focused on whether a given candidate could win or not, and 33% of coverage focused on the process of the campaign in general, while only 11% of coverage concerned issues or policies (Patterson "News Coverage"). As another Shorenstein Center report points out, the "horserace" has always been an important element in US election coverage, especially after 1960 (Patterson "A Tale of Two"). However, recent presidential election cycles have seen the increasing importation of aesthetic markers from sports and game shows into the political sphere as media outlets endeavor to extend the political cycle in order to generate greater amounts of economic and cultural capital. For instance, we might think of the "kids table debates" of the 2016 election cycle, where candidates with low polling numbers held a debate separate from the front runners (Allen). Rather than simply cut these candidates out of the debates altogether, the Fox News producers responsible for the kids table debate evidently felt that viewers, and thus ad-buys, could be garnered by holding the extra debates. These debates also allowed for the production of additional narratives about who might break out into the main debates and so forth. Similarly, in the 2020 cycle, numerous democratic primary debates were held with a large number of candidates participating. Each of these debates generated endless commentary, memes, animated GIFs, and other ancillary coverage. As the political marketplace expands and greater number of candidates invest in political futures, US politics begins to separate from the need to determine who will govern, instead becoming its own engine of images and capital.

## "The Business of America Is Business"

As candidate branding becomes central to the production of political capital, candidates turn to genres of candidacy to establish the frameworks through which they want voters to read their brand. In order to distinguish themselves from other candidates, a candidate will attempt to establish certain themes, policy concerns, or narratives that allow for appeals to different groups of voters. Since his second CEO autobiography, *Surviving at the Top*, Trump has positioned himself as a business candidate with law and order trappings. The business candidate is a particular genre of candidacy that has existed in US political culture since the early twentieth century at least. However, early business candidates like Warren G. Harding and Herbert Hoover pursued the presidency only after having served in government. After the rise of neoliberalism in the 1970s, the business candidate came into greater focus with Iacocca's political feints, the election of oilman turned politician George H.W. Bush, and the successful, populist campaigns of executive Ross Perot. Donald Trump began producing full-fledged political books in the wake of Perot's campaigns, even attempting to secure the nomination of Perot's newly formed Reform Party. After Perot, the Republican Party began to emphasize the business experience of their candidates even more strongly. While George W. Bush was a former governor, he was also an oilman like his father and held an MBA. Other candidates, including nominee Mitt Romney, also pointed to experience in the private sector in developing their campaign ethos. However, Romney's business experience was turned against him and business candidates like Herman Cain and Carly Fiorina floundered. An examination of the representational strategies of neoliberal Republican business candidates will reveal that Trump and Perot succeeded where other business candidates failed because they embraced the simulation of corporate authority produced by images of the heroic manager. Rather than argue that business experience is an asset to assuming the presidency, Perot and Trump treat the presidency as though it is a business position. As a result, they are able to fulfill the cultural desires that yearn for a CEO/President through their command of corporate images.

Like Iacocca, Perot is an important precursor to Trump, in particular because of Perot's synthesis of populist rhetoric and corporate forms and genres, like the CEO autobiography, management book, and infomercial, and his fusion of corporate aesthetics with political forms, like the presidential campaign and the political party. In producing this synthesis, Perot further naturalized the corporate aestheticization of American politics, using corporate images, narratives, and values to reorganize the US political and social future under the commercial rubrics developed by Iacocca and Japanese competition discourse. Where Iacocca's presidential runs never materialized, the popularity of the idea of an Iacocca run suggests that the image of a businessperson as president tantalized a significant portion of the electorate. Ross Perot, a billionaire computer executive, capitalized on this sentiment by running a populist, business-centric campaign that would come to exemplify the business candidate in American politics. Perot ultimately captured 18.9% of the popular vote in the 1992 election, though he polled as high as 39% at various points during the campaign (Ashlock). Perot prepared the ground for Trump's future success by drawing on popular corporate culture to make the argument that a business executive, a person without any government or political experience, would make a viable choice for the presidency. To make this argument, Perot introduces into actual presidential elections the notion that the nation is a corporation, that citizens are shareholders, and that only a businessperson can make America great again. As Perot combines corporate and political genres and forms to make his case, it becomes apparent that what matters in running as a businessperson candidate is not one's autobiography, but one's life production, not that one has been in business, but that one can appear businesslike.

Through his infomercials, his campaign policy books, and his foundation of the Reform Party, Perot reworks Iacocca's notions of "Making America Great Again" and the businessperson presidential candidate for public consumption and use. In the process, Perot reterritorializes the tropes of management literature in order to make the case that someone with no political or government experience is the best candidate to run the government. In 1992's *United We Stand*, Perot claims that "the United States is the largest and most complex business enterprise in the history of mankind," arguing that politicians resist running the government "like a business" because "in business, people are judged on results" (Perot *United* 11). Later on, Perot asks citizens to accept some of the blame for the national debt because "You and I are the shareholders of this country. We own it" (Perot *United* 17). In both of these moments, Perot collapses politics, government, and citizenship under the sign of the corporation. The nation exists as a "business enterprise," ostensibly to generate growth and profit for "the shareholders" or citizens. This framework encourages voters to view politics and civic responsibilities as investments for which they expect a return, an image that reduces the mechanics of politics to the movement of capital and the goal of politics to personal gain.

In a related gesture, in 1996's *My Life & Principles of Success*, Perot dedicates the book "to America's forgotten heroes—*the creators of new businesses*" (Perot *My Life*). Perot follows this dedication with bullet points supporting this figuration, stating, "'Businesses are like people—they are born, mature, grow old, and die," and *"From small acorns mighty oak trees grow!* We must keep planting the seeds to create millions of good jobs in the United States. If we do not create new jobs, even "if our government does everything perfectly...the standard of living will continue to decline for millions of hardworking Americans" (Perot *My Life*). Where *United We Stand* constructs the nation and its citizens as businesslike, *Ross Perot* constructs corporations as humanlike in constitution and organic like trees, a crucial part of the national environment. Without "America's forgotten heroes," the job creators, America will continue its decline. It can only be made great again "in the hands of people who successfully create new companies" (Perot *My Life*). Where *United We Stand* positions citizens as shareholders, *My Life* asks citizen-shareholders to put their trust in heroic manager-politicians like Perot, people who will make the tough decisions to maximize shareholder returns. The rhetoric Perot develops over the course of these two texts does not take into account that shareholders are not created equal, that those with larger investments receive a larger say in company decisions. Perot specifically sings the praises of "people who successfully create new companies." To be successful in business, particularly as it was redefined in the long 1980s, is to maximize profits and growth regardless of the cost. While Perot most likely did not think about this subtext, it is important to note its ramifications, particularly as this corporate reimagining of the US national character gained traction in Perot's wake and began to circulate more widely. As the images circulate and reorganize individuals' understanding of the relationship between the state, citizens, and capital these subtexts begin to form a kind of common sense understanding of why power is arranged in increasingly unequal ways and contribute to the hollowing out of democratic norms.

While George W. Bush had more conventional political experience than Perot, his performance of the president as a heroic manager legitimated some of the practices Trump would adopt. As James P. Pfiffner argues, Bush's status as the "first MBA president" influenced his style of governance. For instance, Bush viewed the role of the president as that of a CEO leading a corporation, making instinctual decisions that a tight team of loyalists then carried out (Pfiffner 3–4). Bush's declaration that he was "the decider" and his claim, "I don't feel that I owe an explanation to anybody" for his decisions as crucial instantiations of Bush's CEO/President conflation (Pfiffner 3–4). While Bush himself did not expect to carry out all of his decisions personally, he repeatedly claimed his position as the symbolic locus of executive branch decision-making. This move undergirds moments like Bush's infamous "mission accomplished" spectacle where Bush parachuted from a plane onto an aircraft carrier. As he touched down, Bush reorganized the collective space of the naval ship around himself as the figure of commander and chief of the military. Although many observers found the "mission accomplished" banner rather premature, the banner underscored Bush's claim to unilateral authority by folding the accomplishment of the mission into the figure of Bush in his military gear while implying that the president's insistence that the job was done was enough to make it so. The "mission accomplished" banner, like Bush's speech in the rubble of the World Trade Center or his famous brush-cutting episodes, produces Bush's life in order to fulfill expectations that blur the line between decisive CEO managing the state and representative figure of the nation's collective will.

While Perot and Bush parlayed their business connections into different types of electoral success, recent presidential candidates with business backgrounds, like Herman Cain, Mitt Romney, and Carly Fiorina, struggled to convert their business experience into political office. I would argue that this struggle is primarily autobiographical in that the narratives that Cain, Romney, and Fiorina produced to justify their move from business to politics read as inauthentic and thus unpersuasive in different ways. As Sidonie Smith argues, political autobiography in the United States relies on "a masculinist mode of bildungsroman," both phallic and narratively linear, to produce political candidates as "authentic," a tendency that Smith labels as "modernist" (Smith 528). The candidate must narrate how they grow to embody the gendered characteristics that voters expect a presidential contender to have. To borrow Bakhtin's formulation, US political autobiography is a narrative "of becoming," in which a candidate's life story culminates on the threshold of the presidency (Bakhtin 20–21). The narrative problem for business candidates becomes to what degree to argue for consonance between business and government and how best to narrate the transition from one sphere to another. For instance, when Iacocca first traced this narrative in his *Autobiography*, he did so by structuring the text to plot carefully the transition from business to politics, following the kind of progressive structure Smith describes. After a linear narrative of Iacocca's life and business dealings, the book transitions to its series of essays. While the essays build up to Iacocca's presidential performance in "Making America Great Again" and a return to his family in the final essay about his wife, he initially eases his way into politics, beginning with an essay on seatbelts and road safety. Both form and genre play a role in Iacocca's case, the structure of the text moving beyond the temporal boundaries of Iacocca's life into a speculative future, while the essay genre presents a persuasive, non-narrative text that more closely resembles a campaign speech. The success of Iacocca's life writing, of course, depended on Iacocca not having to deal with the realities of actually running for president. He was able to produce his own narrative that could stand without inviting real attack.

Other business candidates struggled to produce narratives that fit Smith's description. For instance, Cain's *This is Herman Cain!* released to support his 2012 campaign fails to produce an adequate narrative by framing Cain in purely electoral terms. Cain compounded this failure by playing the political futures market too openly, appearing to do a book tour rather than a political campaign (MacNicol). While Cain's autobiography contains accounts of his childhood and his various business endeavors presented in chronological order, Cain frames the text with his presidential campaign. The text begins with an extended account of Cain's campaign launch and a narrative of his performance in the republican primary debates. The text ends with a chapter that imagines in some detail Cain's first days in office, lingering over descriptions of Cain in the Oval Office. The book's preoccupation with the rituals and trappings of the presidency undercut Cain's claims to be a political outsider—he comes across as too eager to assume the role. Further, in describing his debate performance, campaign announcement, and first day in office, Cain barely mentions his business experience. Instead, he focuses on recounting particular moments from his campaign that elicited positive responses from audiences. As a result, Cain insists too heavily on his performance of candidacy, pushing to the margins the very appeal of his candidacy in the first place.

Senator Mitt Romney's electoral history is more extensive than Cain's, but he has repeatedly struggled to successfully narrate his experience as an executive as Bain Capital, a venture capital firm. For instance, when Romney first ran for office, campaigning against Ted Kennedy for a Massachusetts senate seat, Kennedy's campaign painted Romney as an enemy of the working class, encouraging fired workers from a company Bain had purchased to speak out against Romney (Kahn). This sort of attack, that Romney was a "vulture capitalist," recurred during the 2012 presidential campaign, with even Romney's primary opponents leveling anti-corporate attacks at him (Borchers et al). Perhaps stung by

Kennedy's 18-point victory, Romney's first autobiography *Turnaround* focuses on Romney's work organizing the 2002 Winter Olympics in Salt Lake, rarely mentioning Bain Capital at all. When Romney does discuss Bain in the text, he writes of it in general terms and avoids using it to support his claims to executive ability. Instead, Romney repeatedly emphasizes how successful Bain was and that he was making a considerable sacrifice by walking away from the company. As a result, when Romney makes remarks like, "I kept asking myself, 'Do I really want to stay at Bain Capital for the rest of my life? Do I want to make it even more successful, make even more money? Why?'" his agonizing comes across as elitist and out of touch (Romney *Turnaround* 14). Besides providing him with the means to run, Romney's business experience does not make a persuasive case for Romney as president.

*No Apology* is more successful, linking short, personal anecdotes from Romney's life to policy prescriptions he would tout in his 2012 presidential campaign. The book draws on popular corporate culture and neoliberal discourse more fully than *Turnaround*, beginning, for instance, with Romney standing in line at a Walmart, contemplating how businesses resemble their CEOs, an observation he uses to segue into a discussion of the US founding fathers (Romney *No Apology* 1–2). When Romney invokes Bain in *No Apology*, it is usually to make a point about the importance of data and analysis in decision-making, rather than to argue for the applicability of corporate experience to government (Romney *No Apology* 183–186). As the text progresses, Romney leans on his tenure as governor of Massachusetts, emphasizing his political experience, while explicitly embracing the mainstream Republican party, arguing for its positions as preferable to those of the Democrats. By the end of the book, Romney has narrated himself into his candidacy, but has done so by fitting himself to the political preoccupations of the Republican Party circa 2012. While this undoubtedly helped him to secure the nomination, it also undercuts any claim that a corporate background is particularly beneficial for a would-be president.

Like Romney, Carly Fiorina posed an attractive candidate superficially, but found that her business experience undermined her competitiveness in a crowded field. Fiorina's career at Hewlett Packard could have provided her the ground to paint herself as a strong, heroic manager who could incisively intervene to save America. When she joined HP, Fiorina restructured and reduced the number of the company's internal departments, eliminated profit-sharing for employees in order to institute a commission-based incentive system, and refocused every aspect of the company on profits (Johnson 189–190). In all of her political endeavors, however, Fiorina struggled, like Romney, because she had been the CEO of an actual corporation. Fiorina implemented pay cuts and furloughs at HP before laying off thousands of workers, damaging employee morale, and laying the grounds for her eventual ouster (Johnson 190). The day Fiorina announced her candidacy, a website, CarlyFiorina.org, went live with a display of the number of layoffs Fiorina had presided over (Pagliery). This counter-narrative dogged her campaign, undercutting her ability to make any sort of representative claim. As with Romney, her experience as a CEO, the basic premise of her candidacy, contributed to her loss.

Fiorina's 2015 campaign autobiography, *Rising to the Challenge: My Leadership Journey*, tries to thread a course between emphasizing her business experience and her political experience. She includes a chapter on her ouster from HP, attempting to soften criticism by narrating the betrayal she felt when the board fired her, but the bulk of the book is dedicated to describing her political endeavors. In addition to running for president in 2016, Fiorina unsuccessfully ran for a California senate seat in 2010, served as an advisor to John McCain's 2008 presidential campaign, and accepted a request from George W. Bush to chair the CIA external advisory board from 2007 to 2009 (Fiorina 27). As Fiorina narrates these experiences, weaving in tidbits from her business experience to support her decisions, the effect is to subjugate her organizational knowledge to her political credentials. Indeed, she ends the book by describing how "I got involved in politics when I realized that the policies politicians choose affect our lives in profound ways," invoking the founding fathers and a need to "break free of the persistent narrative that reduces constitutional principles to just the usual battles between Republicans and Democrats" (Fiorina 187). Pointedly absent is any mention of how her experience in corporate America would make her a good candidate to accomplish these things. Instead, like Cain, Fiorina ultimately narrates herself into a politician, positing corporate experience as a background to her candidacy, rather than its motivating force.

The major difference between Donald Trump and other candidates with business backgrounds is that Donald Trump does not rely on being a businessperson to provide the ethos he needs to run for president. Rather, Trump's ethos inheres in acting like people expect a businessperson to act. He fulfills the role that Iacocca developed to convert corporate power into cultural capital. It is important to remember, however, that this role is not an actual management strategy, nor is it connected to actual management experience. Rather, the heroic manager position that Trump imitates is an image, a series of gestures and appearances that fulfill expectations of what corporate power looks like. As we will see in the next half of the chapter, Trump's consistency in iterating this image allows him to generate considerable economic and cultural capital.

## Trump's Futures

Across his three campaign policy books, Trump builds an image of the president as a heroic manager, a singular force of will that can direct the US destiny by itself. Rather than argue that managers could make good presidents, Trump argues that the presidency is a management position, casting politicians and politics as inefficient and inauthentic when compared to a CEO. The contours of Trump's platform are essentially the same as those initially laid out in *Surviving at the Top*. Drawing on narratives rooted in Japanese management discourse, Trump depicts an America threatened by foreign competitors and elitist politicians, besieged by crime, and facing an economic decline. As in the management literature of the 1980s, only a radical reorganization of American government, embodied in the figure of the heroic manager, can meet these challenges. While actual executives like Romney and Fiorina floundered because their management experience read as elitist, Trump instead fulfills the popular image of the CEO originally advanced by Lee Iacocca. Trump senses that what matters is not the experience or skill of management, but the projection of the qualities associated with the symbol of the heroic manager: toughness, strength, straight-talk, and success. As Trump plays the political futures market, releasing campaign books and feinting a candidacy to generate economic and cultural capital, he disseminates an image of the presidency that only he can fulfill.

After Perot's 1996 run for president as the candidate for his newly created Reform Party, dissension spread through the party's ranks. While perennial presidential candidate Pat Buchanan angled for the nomination, there was a groundswell of support to draft Donald Trump as the party's candidate. Trump capitalized on this interest by publically toying with the idea of running for president, eventually rushing to press *The America We Deserve*, a campaign policy book that sought to cash in on the interest in a Trump candidacy. However, Trump ultimately did not run. In 2004's *TRUMP:*

*How to Get Rich*, Trump dedicates less than a page to his flirtation with the presidency, insisting that he simply did not have the time to mount a campaign (Trump *How To* 56–57). Although Trump did not formally run in 2000, *The America We Deserve* modulates his life production to include the campaign book genre, providing the model for Trump's future campaign books, as well as seeding American politics with a more radical vision of the business candidate for president.

As Sidonie Smith argues, authenticity effects are crucial to the life writing of contemporary US politicians (Smith 525). This is why Carly Fiorina discusses her daughter's death and Mitt Romney describes himself shopping at Walmart; part of their texts' performance is to construct a sense of the candidate's "real" self, whether through calculated emotional intimacy or by imitating the daily lives of voters. Rather than stage this kind of performance, Trump instead reframes notions of authenticity, opposing authentic, decisive business with inauthentic, craven politics. Trump uses the consistency of his lifelong performance of being businesslike to contrast himself with politicians whom he describes as being more actor-like than are celebrities. Trump offers an intensification of Iacocca's claim to represent a common sense approach to governance outside of the binary of US politics by hollowing out the notion of politics itself. Trump complains,

> Our current political system discourages truly capable men and women from seeking public office by forcing politicians to live in a fishbowl. A constant need for officeholders to grovel for campaign dollars means the smartest and most able business executives I know would never consider a bid for public office. (Trump *America* 16)

Here, politicians are not "truly capable men and women," but rather people who "live in a fishbowl" and "grovel for campaign dollars." In contrast, Trump describes himself as "a candidate who comes from outside politics" and declares, "I'm not prepackaged. I'm not plastic. I'm not scripted. And I'm not 'handled.' I tell you what I think. It's quite a departure from the usual office-seeking pols" ((Trump *America* 18–19). In Trump's formulation, politicians are dependent on outside observers as well as donations, but also artificial, simply filling a role that someone else has cast them to play. Politics for Trump is recursive, something politicians do in order to be politicians, but divorced from governance, economics, and ability.

By couching this in terms of talent, claiming that the "political system" itself prevents "truly capable" and "the smartest and most able business executives" from pursuing office, Trump reads politics through a neoliberal fetishization of market competition. Thus, Trump implies that the expectations of visibility and accountability inherent to a democratic system function like government regulations, hampering the realization of profit and growth.

By emphasizing this vision of politics, Trump opens up space to redefine government as business. Like Iacocca and Perot, Trump argues that the United States itself is a corporation and the president a CEO. However, Trump intensifies these conceptions by recasting all Americans as businesspeople, all American history as business history. Citing Arthur Schlesinger's *The Cycles of American History*, Trump explains that Schlesinger argued that American history operates on twenty-year cycles, vacillating between "activist government" and "times of privatization" (Trump *America* 61). Trump criticizes Schlesinger on the grounds that "Schlesinger has it only half right" (Trump *America* 61). Trump then subverts Schlesinger's thesis in two ways that reinforce a neoliberal vision of the United States. First, Trump declares, "the American people never go to sleep...Someone's always awake," implying that Schlesinger's cyclical model is inaccurate—the people are always engaged and striving for something better. Then, Trump describes business as the real activism in America. Trump claims,

> The triumph of American business embodies the very spirit of millions of American entrepreneurs. Only a professor could believe that the unleashed creative genius of the American people isn't activism. I say business and work are the featured events of our history—the real story of America. It's what happens at city hall or in the Rose Garden of the White House that's the sideshow. (Trump *America* 63)

Across these passages, Trump makes the case that the truly representative force that binds Americans together, providing for their needs while offering them opportunity, is business itself. Like the politicians, government here exists only to perpetuate itself and outside of the actual life of the nation, "a sideshow" that does not matter. Rather, for Trump, "the triumph of American business," perhaps meaning the primacy of capitalist consumerism in the cultural life of the United States, represents the "millions of American entrepreneurs" themselves a metonym for "the

American people," better than any elected official could. This goes beyond Ronald Reagan or Lee Iacocca's critiques of government waste and inefficiency to reject the representative claims of democratic government altogether. However, because Trump recasts the American people as a vast network of self-sufficient businesspeople, "linking private ambition to social needs" to provide for the nation, Trump positions his reader to identify with him, a billionaire CEO, rather than with politicians and government officials (Trump *America* 62).

Trump undergirds this bid for identification by referring to his previous life production, recontextualizing earlier narratives within the political framework *The America We Deserve* describes. By reiterating these narratives, Trump not only establishes consistency, locating his political ideas in moments that precede the articulation of those ideas, he also reminds readers of their familiarity with his life. Trump relies on this familiarity to produce identification, walking readers through how to understand Trump's experiences as representative of their own. For instance, Trump reminds us of the Wollman Rink chapter from *The Art of the Deal*:

> In my first book, *The Art of the Deal*, I described the fight I had to wage to persuade the city government to allow me to rebuild the city-owned Wollman skating rink in Central Park—at my own expense. My offer to help was opposed for one reason only: City Hall knew that if I took on the job, the difference between my work and the job the city was doing would expose the incompetence of city government. Once I finally embarrassed Mayor Koch and other city officials into letting me do it, even I was shocked at just how ridiculously incompetent the Koch administration turned out to be. (Trump *America* 46)

Trump begins by reminding us that he has told this story before, but reframes the narrative as a "fight I had to wage" against a recalcitrant government. Initially, this move pits Trump's individual "I" against the collective "city government." However, across the sentences, the government goes through a series of metonymic changes, shifting from "the city government," to "City Hall," to "the city," to "Mayor Koch" and "the Koch administration." These shifts in reference create the impression of government's protean, unaccountable nature, transposing responsibility for its opposition to multiple signs set in opposition to Trump's resolute "I." The juxtaposition of Trump's representational stability against the slippery government encourages the identification Trump seeks his readers to perform. Abstracting out from the narrative, Trump writes,

> I learned from this experience just how hard it is for normal, sane, earnest Americans to make their dreams come true when they have to confront mule-headed, but powerful, burons—a buron being defined as a cross between a bureaucrat and a moron. Nice expression, I think. (Trump *America* 47)

Here, Trump makes explicit that his experience is exemplary, an illustration of the struggles "normal, sane, earnest Americans" face when trying to realize their business "dreams." This particular narrative is important because the government resists the efficient, self-funded, public-minded action that the private individual undertakes, thus serving as a demonstration of Trump's insistence that business is better government than government. The moment could be read as an example of how Trump, as a billionaire, operates in a sphere completely separated from average citizens who could not personally fund a municipal project. However, by casting it in these terms, Trump turns his elite status into a point of populist identification.

Trump bowed out of the 2000 Reform Party primary, leaving Buchanan to assume the candidacy, but the populist image he forged in *The America We Deserve* would fuel Trump's on-going political engagement. Trump did not campaign in 2004, the same year he began starring in the reality television show *The Apprentice*. However, *The Apprentice* helped spread Trump's life production to all corners of the US media, dramatizing the heroic manager persona that Trump established in his many books. The intense public interest in Trump's life production would fuel Trump's adoption of Twitter in 2009 and sustain his social media critiques of US President Barack Obama. In turn, this renewed political engagement allowed Trump to make further investments in the presidential futures markets, penning two more successful campaign books before winning the presidency outright.

Scholars have produced considerable excellent work on Trump's use of Twitter and its political, symbolic, and discursive implications.[6] Here, I would like to briefly consider how Trump's Twitter usage, particularly his use of Twitter to advance the "Birther" conspiracy against Obama, reinforced Trump's political life production, paving the way for his 2012 and 2015 campaign books. While scholars have considered the racist, xenophobic content of the birther conspiracy, there are structural elements to Trump's use of Twitter to attack Obama that are important to understand. As with *The Apprentice*, Twitter served as a platform for Trump to extend his life production, metastasizing his image throughout political and cultural discourse. As a medium, Twitter reinforces the populist executive image that Trump constructed in *The America We Deserve* because the brevity and public nature of the medium grants tweets a sense of being transparent, immediate, and authentic (Polak 78). Because of his large following, Trump was able to amplify what political scientist Michael Barkun calls "fringe" ideas, establishing the birther conspiracy in mainstream political discourse (Barkun 439). As Stephanie Kelley-Romano and Kathryn Carew argue, the birther conspiracy provided the discursive infrastructure for Trump to make further accusations against Obama, even after Obama released his long-form birth certificate (Polak 41). For instance, Sara Polak points out that Trump politicized the Ebola scare of 2014, using the opportunity to call Obama "weak" while criticizing his leadership (Polak 78). As Polak argues, Twitter's appearance of democracy validated Trump's voice while allowing him to construct a discourse intended to pit the nation against its president (Polak 77). I would argue that Twitter allowed Trump a space in which he could invest his life production with a sense of transparency and democracy while constructing Obama as secretive and authoritarian. The point of this discourse was not solely to discredit or diminish Obama, but rather to articulate a radical vision of the presidency and its powers. Obama's response to Trump was designed to silence his attacks. However, both the release of Obama's birth certificate and his roasting of Trump at the White House correspondents' dinner legitimated Trump's position as a populist business candidate by recognizing his voice and responding to it. When Trump released *Time to Get Tough* in December of 2011, seven months after he dropped out of the 2012 race, he cashed in on this legitimacy.

Throughout *Time to Get Tough*, Trump focuses his attacks on President Barack Obama, blaming him for a host of ills that Trump claims America faces. Through the course of these attacks, Trump constructs Obama as weak and incompetent, a self-serving politician who contrasts sharply with tough, able, pragmatic businesspeople like Trump. At the same time, however, Trump invests the figure of Obama with considerable power, arguing that the president alone bears responsibility for any number of poor decisions while implying that Obama could have easily effected different outcomes if he had been so inclined. At the beginning of the text, Trump writes,

> If we keep on this path, if we reelect Barack Obama, the America we leave our kids and grandkids won't look like the America we were blessed to grow up in. The American Dream will be in hock. The shining city on the hill will start to look like an inner-city wreck. It won't be morning in America, as President Reagan put it. We'll be mourning for America, an America that was lost on Obama's watch. (Trump *Time To* 4)

Here, the fate of the nation is yoked to whether Obama is reelected or not in a move that ignores both party politics and the legislative branch of the US government. The problem is not progressive policies as such, but the fact that they are Obama's policies. Trump similarly ignores the fact that the Republicans controlled both the House and the Senate, exerting considerable influence on what actions Obama could undertake. Instead, Obama can change the "look" of America, driving up the debt until the nation's spirit is pawned and the country crumbles into a dying "wreck." While these images are born out of a desire to paint Obama as incompetent, they imply that the presidency itself is powerful enough to make these drastic changes unilaterally. This image of the presidency, that the president themselves has the power to make America great again, forms the core of Trump's eventual successful presidential run.

Trump uses the figure of Obama to construct an image of the presidency as a position for a heroic manager who can single-handedly make or break the nation. In doing so, Trump draws on the images of America as a land of businesspeople that he established in *The America We Deserve*. According to Trump, Obama's alleged incompetence is a function of his lack of business experience: "He may have been a good 'community organizer,' but the man is a lousy international dealmaker. This is hardly a surprise—he's never built or run a business in his life" (Trump *Time To* 5). Going back to *The Art of the Deal*, Trump's life production centers on "deal making," both in terms of content (his autobiographies focus on the various deals he's made) and in terms of form (each text is structured as a discrete series of deals). By painting Obama as a "lousy international dealmaker," Trump advances a metric of measuring a president's effectiveness that only Trump can most effectively fulfill. In doing so, Trump casts presidential fitness not as adherence to a particular set of policies or even to the possession of a certain background, but rather as a matter of image and personality. Trump writes,

> If we get tough and make the hard choices, we can make America a rich nation—and respected—once again. The right president can actually make America money by brokering big deals. We don't always think of our presidents as jobs and business negotiators, but they are. Presidents are our dealmakers in chief. But the outcome of a deal is only as effective as the person brokering it. (Trump *Time To* 4)

Trump describes America's national goals as getting "rich," "making money," and earning "respect" by being "tough," goals that Trump's life production implies he knows how to reach.

The ability to achieve these goals is not a matter of priorities, alliances, or compromise. Rather America can only be successful if it has "the right president," since negotiations as "only as effective as the person brokering it." This emphasis places the onus for America's success on the person of the president themselves, rather than on ideological positions or political skill. As Trump insists,

> Some people think the presidency no longer matters, that the United States is finished. But let me tell you, the president makes all the difference in the world. If we get the right president, our country can become stronger and better and more successful than ever before. (Trump *Time To* 183)

By insisting, "the president makes all the difference," Trump reduces a host of political contingencies to an exercise in personality, seeking to advance a vision in which the presidency inheres in surfaces and appearances. We might think here of the passage quoted above where Trump uses the verb "look" twice to indicate how Obama's reelection will change America—it will "look" different than it supposedly should; it will "look" like something else. Part of the verb use is a racist dog whistle, drawing on stereotypes of "the inner-city," to use Trump's words, as a racially and economically Othered space, as well as the myriad racist attacks on Obama, the US first Black president. The verb use also points to Trump's preoccupation with appearances, a concern he brings to his conception of the presidency as well. By reducing the presidency to appearance, Trump intensifies the cultural vision of the president as CEO.

Trump recognizes the metonymic relationship between president and nation, but reads it through the lens of his own executive experience, collapsing distinctions between the part and the whole. In Trump's cosmology, the United States is white, straight, male, and entrepreneurial. Indeed, Trump says as much, arguing that the president "can help create an environment that allows the rest of us—entrepreneurs, small businessmen, big businessmen—to make America rich" (Trump *Time To* 8). Trump's America is a recursive loop. The "businessmen" "make America rich," but these same businessmen are "the rest of us" that the president governs. Since the businessmen are America, they make America rich by enriching themselves. The president, chosen as a representative figure, must therefore be a self-enriching businessman himself.

Where business candidates like Romney and Fiorina treat corporate experience as a background one can translate into government, Trump embraces Perot's conception of the nation as a corporation where corporate experience is all that one needs to govern. Where Perot's image of the United States was general, however, Trump specifically envisions the United States as a version of the Trump Organization. Trump writes,

> My primary reason for running for the presidency would be to straighten out the mess Obama has made of our country. I have built a truly great company, one with unbelievable assets and locations that I believe are about as good as it gets. We have great asset value, cash flow, and very little debt. I want the American people to see this, because ultimately our country is, in a certain way, the exact opposite of my company. (Trump *Time To* 179)

Superficially, the United States seems to be the opposite of the Trump Organization because it does not have "asset value" or "cash flow" and carries considerable debt. However, if the nation is the opposite of the Organization as described here, it is also not "truly great" and it might be "as bad as it gets." This opposition hinges on the Obama/Trump binary that drives *Time to Get Tough*, implying that the poor state of the nation and the great state of the Trump Organization result from the work of their respective executives. One of the representational effects of the image of the heroic manager is that as corporate action collapses in the figure of the manager, the particularities of the work of management flatten, assuming a gestural character. When Romney or Fiorina produce their candidacies, they use their political experience to stage the move from one sphere to another. Trump, however, makes no distinction between the work of a president and the work of a CEO, a tendency that reaches its full expression in this passage. As a result, if we follow Trump's logic, assuming that he "straightens out the mess," the United States would "have great asset value, cash flow, and very little debt," and Donald Trump as its executive—it would become the Trump Organization.

Ironically, Trump offers in *Time to Get Tough* an intensification of Obama's own use of media and image to secure the presidency in 2008. While Obama campaigned on an idealistic, progressive platform embodied in the candidate himself and then governed more pragmatically, Trump seeks in the text to eliminate the distinction between the surface-oriented campaign and actual governance. The right-wing media's anti-Obama imaginary swarmed with contradictory images of Obama as a weak authoritarian or a typical politician who was Other and outside "normal" American values. Trump uses the structure of these images alongside a parody of Obama's 2008 "hope and change" platform to reinforce cultural images of the president as a personality and a force, a heroic manager whose image concretizes "America's power and dominance in the world" (Trump *Crippled* 190). When Trump ran again in 2016, the ability to fulfill Trump's vision of the presidency, a vision that essentially posits Trump as president in the first place, became central to the race for the republican nomination, allowing Trump to defeat easily the more typical politicians against whom he ran.

Trump released *Crippled America* in November 2015 as part of his presidential campaign. The book would go on to become one of Trump's best-selling works, moving hundreds of thousands of copies while spending thirteen weeks on the *New York Times* Best-Seller List (Newman). Much of *Crippled America*'s political prescriptions mirror those of *Time to Get Tough*, including wall building, going after China for currency manipulation, cutting taxes, and increasing military spending. The primary differences in the two texts emerge from the context of *Crippled America*'s publication. When Trump announced his run in 2015, he descended the escalator in Trump Tower and made his now infamous speech in which he claimed undocumented immigrants were rapists and criminals. Because of this speech, NBC fired Trump from *The Apprentice*, leaving him in need of a new venture. Just as *Crippled America* resembles *Time to Get Tough*, it seems plausible that Trump's 2016 run meant to mirror his 2012 run, with Trump bowing out strategically after generating capital from a new campaign book and his on-going television series. The combination of losing his *Apprentice* gig while generating increased interest in his books and image probably contributed to Trump staying in and eventually winning the race.

While *Crippled America's* policy positions mimic those of *Time to Get Tough*, the text differs in its tone and method of attack. Where *Time to Get Tough* is aggressive and angry, *Crippled America* is bleak and dark. The failing America of *Time to Get Tough* has failed, leaving a desolate shell of a country in its place. *Time to Get Tough* constructs Trump against the figure of Obama, but Obama goes largely unnamed in *Crippled America*. Instead, Trump constructs himself as a builder, someone who can salvage and restore the past into a new and better version of itself. A crucial image for *Crippled America* comes from the narrative of the conversion of the Commodore Hotel into the Grand Hyatt, a story Trump originally related in *The Art of the Deal*. Trump writes, "The exterior of the Commodore was filthy, and the inside was so dark and dingy that it felt like the building was on the verge of becoming a welfare hotel. It was a dying building, in a dying neighborhood, in a struggling city" (Trump *Crippled* 159). The exterior of the Commodore, seen from the outside, matches the building's interior, a place so decrepit that Trump thinks it is in danger of becoming temporary housing for people on government assistance. The building also stands in as a metonym for both its neighborhood and New York City in the 1970s, "the once great Commodore Hotel," now a decaying sign of the city's decline (Trump *Crippled* 159). Trump claims, "When I looked at the Commodore, I saw its potential…I had a vision of what could be done" (Trump *Crippled* 160). Trump then describes the process of constructing the Grand Hyatt:

> There were detractors all along the way. For instance, the preservationists were angry about my creating a new and beautiful glass exterior façade. Inside, I gutted all of the floors and replaced them with the best available materials. The hotel, the Grand Hyatt, has been successful since the day it opened in 1980. It became the foundation for the restoration of the entire Grand Central neighborhood as well as my calling card—introducing the Trump quality brand to the people of New York. The project marked the first time I took a large-scale failing property and made it great again…I've done it over and over again in the thirty-five years since—and now for the really big and important one: our country. (Trump *Crippled* 161)

The Grand Hyatt goes from being a symbol of Trump's iconoclasm to being a metaphor for Trump's vision of the presidency, an image of revitalization, investment, and reflection. Trump replaces the "filthy" exterior of the Commodore with the Grand Hyatt's reflective "glass façade," remodeling the interior of the building to remake it as his "calling card." On the surface, as a metaphor for the United States, the Grand Hyatt seems promising. Just as Ronald Reagan reworked John Winthrop's biblical "city on a hill" to a "shining city on a hill," emphasizing an outward action, a sense of agency, not present in the original, Trump reworks Reagan through the lens of neoliberalism, constructing his own symbol of America as a lustrous luxury hotel that bears his imprimatur.

Read against the grain, however, the Grand Hyatt as a metaphor for the United States encodes an authoritarian view of the presidency. The narrative emphasizes the "gutting" of the building and its new façade, an aesthetic decision that both rejected convention and associated the building with Trump Tower, which has a similar façade designed by the same architect. Rather than compromise on the design or tailor the building to fit its surroundings, decisions that would require recognition of different viewpoints and priorities, Trump remakes the building in his own image and dismisses "the detractors." In addition, the building becomes Trump's "calling card," a symbol for him to deploy in situations (much like this one) as a sign of his own ability. Trump is not concerned with the experience of people working or staying in the hotel, but rather its utility for expanding his brand and generating him capital. This is an intensification of the image of the United States as the Trump Organization in *Time to Get Tough*, only here the nation is not an organization, a collective entity at least in theory, but a "large-scale failing property." As we reach the end of the passage, having envisioned the shift from the derelict Commodore to the sparkling Grand Hyatt, the metaphor breaks as we realize that while Trump's vision for America might be the Grand Hyatt, his vision of America is the "filthy," "dingy" Commodore, dark and decrepit inside and out.

Throughout the passage, Trump emphasizes his "I." He is the subject that performs the verbs that "made [the Commodore] great again." While the city on a hill metaphor has always been corporate, an image of a community bound together in the act of being a community, Trump's Grand Hyatt is remarkably singular, a monument to one person, built by one person's actions. At first, this seems unpersuasive. However, the image is in keeping with how in

US culture we have come to understand the work of organizations. The CEO, like Bill Gates, Steve Jobs, or Lee Iacocca, stands as the face and force of the corporation they built. While, for instance, the Microsoft Corporation undoubtedly emerged out of the collective actions and decisions of many different people, there is a cultural sense that its existence and that of Bill Gates intertwine. Because of what Mayr and Siri call "the symbolizing effect" of the heroic manager, an effect heightened by the ubiquity of popular corporate culture, we readily assume that someone like Trump is speaking metonymically, substituting his "I" for the actions of many (Mayr and Siri 174). However, this "I" threatens to take on a life of its own, erasing the collective work that underwrites it. Just as in the Grand Hyatt passage Trump can assert that he removed and replaced the floors, but the names and lives of the people who actually performed that labor would be difficult, if not possible to recover.

Over the course of nearly thirty years, Trump carved out a niche in the presidential field that only he could fill. Romney, Fiorina, and other business candidates use the bildungsroman model of the campaign autobiography, attempting to narrate themselves into the presidency. However, this merely opens up for the public the possibility of someone like them becoming president. The narrative compromises these non-populist business candidates make to demonstrate their political and cultural fitness for office ultimately undermine the case for their candidacies. While Trump's policies shift over time to a degree, the core of his perpetual candidacy remains the same: the presidency should be viewed as a role for a heroic manager who eschews political norms and brings corporate experience to the White House. Trump's early flirtations with the presidency seem absurd on the surface, but the consistency with which he presents his candidacy as well as its consonance with his interminable life production produces a sense of possibility, even inevitability by the time Trump finally found himself under conditions where he was forced to see the whole thing through. Rather than watch a candidate grow into the office, we grew to read the presidency through the lens Trump offered.

## Conclusion

The point of playing a futures market is not necessarily to deliver the commodity for which one has purchased contracts, but rather to profit from fluctuations in public desire for the commodity. Lee Iacocca, followed by Ross Perot, proved that there was a desire for a populist business candidate and developed strategies for performing that candidacy. Popular corporate culture's infection of electoral politics, exemplified in the campaign memoir boom, creates a market where this kind of candidate can thrive. While politicians had to learn that they could generate capital by floating candidacies in mass-market books, CEOs had been making those moves for decades. Unlike politicians, who had to use discourse drawn from corporate culture to legitimate their ideas, CEOs (real and pretend) already embodied that discourse without the need for translation. While candidates like Romney, Cain, and Fiorina appear novel for their business backgrounds, they are behind the times, rehearsing shopworn translation techniques that simply encode them as typical politicians. Trump understood that the market was about desire. Just as he would try out different slogans at his rallies, testing them and repeating the ones that generate the best response, Trump sought to give people the candidate they wanted, fulfilling a desire he himself had helped to kindle.

Although it is possible that Trump did not actually intend to win the nomination or the presidency, like the futures trader whose contract comes due, Trump delivered the commodity he had pledged to supply. Throughout his presidency, he performed the role of the heroic manager, acting as though he alone was responsible for the actions of the government while pretending that only the desires of his most ardent supporters mattered. Like the heroic manager, Trump's performance merely masked the system churning behind him, most of the labor of his administration done by other people using him as cover their ideological ends. Trump for his part was mostly interested in continuing his campaign, even declaring his 2020 candidacy on the day of his inauguration so he could begin raising money right away. In a sense, he turned around and began playing the futures market again, seeking to generate economic and cultural capital off the presidency itself. While this might seem crass, it represents the logical end game of the financialization of politics. After all, if running for president can be made lucrative, being president offers even more opportunities to enrich oneself.

## Notes

1 Political marketing is its own discipline, see: Pitch, Christopher, "Evolution of Political Branding: Typologies, Diverse Settings and Future Research," *Journal of Political Marketing*, vol. 19, 2020: 3–14.
2 On mindfulness as "capitalist spirituality" see: Purser, Ronald, *McMindfulness: How Mindfulness Became the New Capitalist Spirituality*. Repeater Press, 2019.

3 I mean this here in both the sense that money has come to drive US politics and the sense that politics has assumed the logics of finance: investing, speculating, hedging, and so forth, as well as a decoupling of the signs of politics (like the campaign autobiography) from politics itself.

4 On Ryan, see: Francisco, Timothy, "Futuristic Nostalgia: Tim Ryan's *Healing America*," *American Literary History* "Presidential Campaign Autobiographies 2020" Supplement, 2019: e33–e41.

5 See, for instance: "I'm Kirsten Gillibrand." YouTube, uploaded by Kirsten Gillibrand, 27 Jun. 2019, https://www.youtube.com/watch?v=ACuUSppHc4M.

6 See, for instance: Ouyang, Yu and Richard Waterman, *Trump, Twitter, and the American Democracy: Political Communication in the Digital Age*. Palgrave, 2020; Ott, Brian L., "The age of Twitter: Donald J. Trump and the Politics of Debasement," *Critical Studies in Media Communication*, vol. 34, no. 1 (2017): 59–68; Lockhart, Michele, Ed., *President Donald Trump and His Political Discourse: Ramifications of Rhetoric via Twitter*. Routledge, 2019.

## Works Cited

Allen, Jonathan. "It Was Brutal to be in the 'Kids' Table' Debate." *Vox*, 6 Aug. 2015, https://www.vox.com/2015/8/6/9114283/kids-table-Republican-debate-brutal.

Ashlock, Alex and Jeremy Hobson. "How Ross Perot's Third Party Presidential Bids Shook Up American Politics." *wbur*, 10 Jul. 2019, https://www.wbur.org/hereandnow/2019/07/10/perot-third-party-presidential-bids.

Bakhtin, Mikhail. "The Bildungsroman." *Speech Genres and Other Essays*, translated by Vern W. McGee, edited by Caryl Emerson and Michael Holquist. University of Texas Press, 2007.

Banet-Weiser, Sarah. *Authentic$^{TM}$: The Politics of Ambivalence in a Brand Culture*. NYU Press, 2012.

Barkun, Michael. "President Trump and the 'Fringe'." *Terrorism and Political Violence*, vol. 29, no. 3, 2017, pp. 437–443.

Borchers, Tyler and Jerry L. Miller. "Bain & Political Capital in the 2012 GOP Primary Debates." *American Behavioral Scientist*, vol. 58, no. 4, 2014, pp. 574–590.

Cassidy, John. "Only Republican Voters Can Stop Donald Trump Now." *The New Yorker*, 15 Jan. 2016, https://www.newyorker.com/news/john-cassidy/only-republican-voters-can-stop-donald-trump-now.

CBS Staff. "Donald Trump Officially Fired from 'The Celebrity Apprentice'." *CBS News*, 13 Aug. 2015, https://www.cbsnews.com/news/donald-trump-officially-fired-from-the-celebrity-apprentice/.

Ellis, Richard J. and Mark Dedrick. "The Presidential Candidate, Then and Now." *Perspectives on Political Science*, vol. 26, no. 4, 1997, pp. 208–216.

Fehrman, Craig. "Reagan and the Rise of the Blockbuster Political Memoir." *American Literary History*, vol. 24, no. 3, pp. 468–490.

Fiorina, Carly. *Rising to the Challenge*. Penguin Publishing, 2015.
Francisco, Timothy. "Futuristic Nostalgia: Tim Ryan's *Healing America*." *American Literary History* vol. 32, no. 2, "Presidential Campaign Autobiographies 2020" Supplement, 2020, pp. e33–e41.
Gillibrand, Kirsten. "I'm Kirsten Gillibrand." *YouTube*, uploaded by Kirsten Gillibrand, 27 Jun. 2019, https://www.youtube.com/watch?v=ACuUSppHc4M.
Johnson, Craig. "The Rise and Fall of Carly Fiorina." *Journal of Leadership & Organizational Studies*, vol. 15, no. 2, 2008, pp. 188–196.
Kahn, Joseph. "An Untidy Private Life, Then a Turn to Stability." *Boston Globe*, 19 Feb. 2009.
Li, Stephanie. "Elizabeth Warren's *A Fighting Chance*." *American Literary History* vol. 32, no. 2, "Presidential Campaign Autobiographies 2020" Supplement, 2020, pp. e50–e57.
Li, Stephanie and Gordon Hunter. "Introduction: Writing the Presidency." *American Literary History*, vol. 24, no. 3, 2012, pp. 419–423.
Lockhart, Michele, Ed. *President Donald Trump and His Political Discourse: Ramifications of Rhetoric via Twitter*. Routledge, 2019.
MacNicol, Glynnis. "Is It Possible Herman Cain Is Only Pretending to Run for President?" *Business Insider*, 24 Oct. 2011, https://www.businessinsider.com/herman-cain-book-tour-president-2011-10.
Mayr, Katharina and Jasmin Siri. "Management as a Symbolizing Construction? Re-Arranging the Understanding of Management." *Historical Social Research*, vol. 36, no. 1, 2011, pp. 160–179.
Newman, Rick. "If Book Sales Were Votes, Donald Trump Would be President." *Yahoo! Finance*, 9 Mar. 2016, https://www.yahoo.com/amphtml/finance/news/if-book-sales-were-votes--donald-trump-would-be-president-151742659.html.
Ott, Brian L. "The Age of Twitter: Donald J. Trump and the Politics of Debasement." *Critical Studies in Media Communication*, vol. 34, no. 1, 2017, pp. 59–68.
Ouyang, Yu and Richard Waterman. *Trump, Twitter, and the American Democracy: Political Communication in the Digital Age*. Palgrave, 2020.
Pagliery, Jose. "Ouch! CarlyFiorina.org Shows Her Layoffs at HP." *CNN*, 5 May 2015, https://money.cnn.com/2015/05/04/technology/carly-fiorina-website/index.html.
Patterson, Thomas E. "News Coverage of the 2016 Presidential Primaries: Horse Race Reporting Has Consequences." Shorenstein Center, 11 Jul. 2016, https://shorensteincenter.org/news-coverage-2016-presidential-primaries/.
Patterson, Thomas E. "A Tale of Two Elections: CBS and Fox News' Portrayal of the 2020 Presidential Campaign." Shorenstein Center, 17 Dec. 2020, https://shorensteincenter.org/patterson-2020-election-coverage/.
C-Span. "Perot Campaign Commercial 1992." *CSpan*, 30 Oct. 1992, https://www.c-span.org/video/?34277-1/perot-campaign-commercial-1992.

Perot, Ross. *My Life & The Principles for Success.* Summit Publishing Group, 1996.
Perot, Ross. *United We Stand: How We Can Take Back Our Country.* Hyperion, 1992.
Pfiffner, James P. "The First MBA President: George W. Bush as Public Administrator." *Public Administration Review* vol. 67, no. 1, January/February, 2007, pp. 6–20.
Pitch, Christopher. "Evolution of Political Branding: Typologies, Diverse Settings and Future Research." *Journal of Political Marketing*, vol. 19, 2020, pp. 3–14.
Polak, Sara. "'#Unpresidented': The Making of the First Twitter President." *Violence and Trolling on Social Media: History, Affect, and Effects of Online Vitriol*, edited by Sara Polak and Daniel Trottier. Amsterdam University Press, 2020, pp. 65–86.
Purser, Ronald. *McMindfulness: How Mindfulness Became the New Capitalist Spirituality.* Repeater Press, 2019.
Roberts, Wendy Raphael. "Polly's Girl: The Cruel Maternalism of Kirsten Gillibrand's *Off the Sidelines*." *American Literary History*, vol. 32, no. 2, "Presidential Campaign Autobiographies 2020" Supplement, 2020, pp. e17–24.
Romney, Mitt. *No Apology: Believe in America.* St. Martin's Griffin, 2012.
Romney, Mitt. *Turnaround: Crisis, Leadership, and the Olympic Games.* Regnery Publishing, 2004.Smith, Sidonie. "'America's Exhibit A': Hillary Rodham Clinton's *Living History* and the Genres of Authenticity." *American Literary History*, vol. 24, no. 3, 2012, pp. 523–542.
Trump, Donald. *Crippled America: How to Make America Great Again.* Simon & Schuster, 2015.
Trump, Donald and Dave Shiflett. *The America We Deserve.* Renaissance Books, 2000.
Trump, Donald and Meredith McIver. *How to Get Rich.* Random House, 2004.
Trump, Donald and Wynton Hall, Peter Schweizer, and Meredith McIver. *Time to Get Tough: Making America #1 Again.* Regnery Publishing, 2011.
Voelz, Johannes. "Towards an Aesthetics of Populism, Part I: The Populist Space of Appearance." *Yearbook of Research in English and American Literature (REAL)*, vol. 34, 2018, pp. 203–228.

# 5   Coda: No More Bullshit
## Trump Signs Off

One of the aesthetically disarming aspects of the photographs of the January 6, 2021, attack on the US Capitol building is the sheer mass of people. Crammed in close together, the thousands of people surrounding the building become indistinguishable from one another, a writhing mass of camouflage, red hats, American flags, and giant banners proclaiming "TRUMP 2020 NO MORE BULLSHIT" and "KEEP AMERICA GREAT." The crowd flows against the building, moving like a liquid, eventually forcing their way inside. The unbounded and indistinguishable flow of Trump supporters recalls Baudrillard's description of the "ecstasy of communication," a schizophrenic subjectivity "characterized…by the absolute proximity to and total instantaneousness with things" (Baudrillard 27). The boundaries between subject and object disappear as the subject is no longer able to "produce the limits of [their] very being," instead becoming "a pure screen, a pure absorption and resorption surface of the influent networks" (Baudrillard 27). Hyped up on Parler posts, organized on private social media groups, communicating through encrypted chat apps, lost in right-wing media's metastatic assertion that the election was stolen, moving forward at Trump's command to "stop the steal," the Capitol insurrectionists were not just a flow of human beings, but a flow of a data and misinformation, produced by, around, and through Donald Trump. At a speech that afternoon, Trump rehearsed a long litany of conspiracies about the supposedly stolen election, telling the crowd "we're going to walk down to the Capitol," while reassuring them, "I'll be there with you" ("Transcript of Trump's Speech"). Trump did not walk down to the Capitol, but he went with them, nonetheless. In the wake of the attack, many condemned Trump for inciting the protestors, for producing them through a long process of shaping the data that makes up their lives. At the same time, however, as the flow of people, decked out in Make America Great Again (MAGA) clothing, hung a Trump flag outside of the Capitol, it was clear that these people produced Trump as much as he produced them by investing their time, lives, and money into his life production. In a way, what these photographs capture in the teeming crowd is "a pure screen" filled with Trump's managerial image.

The Capitol insurrectionists cast themselves as revolutionaries, but theirs was a mock revolution, another screen with another image, the specter of a leveraged buyout. As Jeffrey Nealon describes, the ramping up of neoliberalism in the 1980s required casting off older theories of the firm, exchanging a preoccupation with slow, steady growth that benefitted managers and laborers, for "efficient" Just In Time capitalism where the only goals are growth and shareholder profit (Nealon 17–18). This was a revolution, as Nealon puts it, "the revolt of the rich," which resulted in "the upward distribution of wealth to CEOs and shareholders" at the expense of everyone else (Nealon 18–19). From that point on, there was no move beyond, but only an intensification of these effects (Nealon 20). The Capitol attackers acted as shareholders angered at the actions of Congress' management, attempting to break apart a structure that, in their eyes, refused to pay their dividends. At the same time, however, they acted like capital, flowing freely into the seat of government, attempting to rearrange the organization of power in favor of Trump, the corporation, unmuzzled by the Citizens United Supreme Court decision that ruled that money is speech. Their attempted takeover of the Capitol failed, however, because, like Trump winning the presidency, once they got inside, they did not know what to do. Instead, reflecting Trump, they produced images of action, made aborted threats, and attempted to frame themselves as heroes. In the course of this, they supplied the free flow of data that made their capture possible, even inevitable.

In the media coverage that followed the insurrection, photographs of many of the suspects appeared, gleaned from social media, and circulated to the nation's screens. I recall one photograph in particular in which an individual poses in front of a television, in one hand a grayscale American flag with one blue stripe, a sign of pro-police sentiment, and in the other hand a shotgun. This man, dressed in black, pulls a kind of yawning, yelling face, looking directly into the camera. Trump's face beams out from the screen behind him (Hurler et al.). The photograph, probably produced for social media, is a kind of life production. What we see is not the life this man has lived, but the life he wants to live, a hypermasculine, militarized version of Trump's heroic manager, unable to distinguish between the objects that make him feel powerful, the flag, the gun, his screens, and his own subject position. As people like this were arrested, the media juxtaposed these life-producing images with their mugshots, the kind of institutional photography designed to strip away one's subjectivity. Many of the rioters had even shaved their beards before their mugshots, giving them an additional aura of vulnerability as they slipped seamlessly from their sense of subjecthood, revolutionaries fighting tyranny, to the objecthood of incarceration and media-circulated imagery.

Many hoped for something similar for Trump, a desire encoded both in four years of fantasies of Trump having to be dragged out of the White House and now two attempts to impeach him. These are hopes for Trump to be reduced to an object, something that can be discarded and forgotten. Indeed, the major social media companies achieved something of this effect by deplatforming Trump, a move that made a meme out of Trump's deactivated Twitter. It does not seem likely that a full symbolic reckoning is possible, however. The irony of overrunning the US Capitol in the name of democracy was lost on the insurrectionists precisely because Trump has taught them to eschew symbolic depth. The American flag has thirteen stripes that stand in for the thirteen original colonies, fifty stars that stand for fifty states. A Trump flag says "TRUMP" on it. If it has stars, they are just stars. There is no subtext. Trump, for his part, will not change. After all, the same strategies he described in 1988 in *The Art of the Deal*, of avoiding personal risk by playing sources of capital off of one another, are the same strategies he used to attempt to extend his political power. He claimed to have won an election he lost because presidents who lose their elections generally lose leadership of their parties. By playing his voters as capital off of the Republican Party's fear of losing their own power, he retained ownership of that massive flow of people he produced and who in turn produce him.

I would like to end with the image of Trump's final take off in Air Force One as Frank Sinatra's "My Way," spilled from the speakers, over the crowd. In this final moment of his presidency, Trump returns to the aesthetics and life production techniques I have sought to describe in this book. At his rallies, talking about how he improvised the slogan, "drain the swamp," Trump liked to talk about Frank Sinatra and "My Way": "You know, great, great singers, a lot of great artists, great singers, Frank Sinatra. So Frank Sinatra didn't like My Way when he first sang it. And then he noticed the audience like it a lot, and then it went out, became number one like big. And all of a sudden he started to love that song My Way, right? So drain the swamp" (Schneider and Eitelmann 42). In this bit, Trump conflates Sinatra and "My Way," suggesting that each one is known for the other, a kind of mutual signature. In this way, "My Way" stands in for the kind of quality Trump frequently calls "genius," as in his discussion of Sylvester Stallone (Trump *Art of the Deal* 34). Like Trump, Sinatra gives his audience what they want, finding "love" in the exchange. However, when Trump lifts off to "My Way" in the wake of the Capitol insurrection under the cloud of a second impeachment and the inauguration of a President Trump attempted to delegitimize, the song's iconoclasm reads both as absurdity and as authenticity. Trump skipped the inauguration on January 20, leaving early reportedly so he would not have to ask Joe Biden if he could use Air Force One. By appropriating both Sinatra's iconic song and Biden's plane, a mark of his office, Trump manages to use stolen signatures to make his own mark.

## Works Cited

Baudrillard, Jean. *The Ecstasy of Communication.* Verso, 1988.
Hurler, Ana, Sarah Macaraeg, Daniel Connolly, Cassandra Stephenson, Travis Dorman, and Rachel Wegner. "What We Know about Eric Muchel of Nashville, Accused 'Zip Tie Guy' in Capitol Riot." *Tennessean*, 1 Oct. 2021.
Nealon, Jeffrey. *Post-Postmodernism or, The Cultural Logic of Just-In-Time Capitalism.* Stanford University Press, 2012.
Schneider, Ulrike and Matthias Eitelmann. *Linguistic Inquiries into Donald Trump's Language: From 'Fake News' to 'Tremendous Success.'* Bloomsbury Publishing, 2020.
"Transcript of Trump's Speech at Rally before US Capitol Riot." *US News*, 13 Jan. 2021.

# Index

Allen, Woody 35
autobiography (genre) 8–9

Bakhtin, Mikhail 40, 85
Baudrillard, Jean 106
Blanchard, Kenneth 54
Bloomberg, Michael 25, 44
Bradford, David 31, 36
Bush, George H. W. 82
Bush, George W. 82, 84–85

Cain, Herman 77, 82, 85–86, 102
campaign autobiography (genre) 76–79, 85, 89–101
Capitol Insurrection 106–109
CEO autobiography (genre) 12, 25–26, 31–32, 37–43, 45, 48, 56–58
Chrysler Corporation 39–40, 47
Citizens United 3, 107
Clinton, Bill 48
Clinton, Hillary 13, 78, 80
Cohen, Allan 31, 36
corporate speech 2–4, 10–12, 30, 38–40
corporate personhood 6–7, 9, 15, 76

De Man, Paul 8–9
DeJoy, Louis 69
Deming, W. Edwards 53
Democratic Party 57, 59
DeSantis, Ron 14–15

Fiorina, Carly 17, 82, 85, 87–90, 97, 101–102
Fox News 81

Gates, Bill 101
General Electric 16, 69
Germany 70
Gillibrand, Kirsten 77, 80
The Grand Hyatt 99–101

Harding, Warren G. 82
heroic manager 17, 26–28, 31, 36–39, 45, 57, 60–61, 69–73, 89, 95, 97, 101–102, 107
Hitler, Adolph 73
Hoover, Herbert 82

Icahn, Carl 69
Iacocca, Lee 35, 39–40, 42–43, 47–54, 56–62, 65, 67–68, 71–72, 76, 78–79, 82, 86, 89, 92, 101

Japan 47, 50–55, 59, 62, 64, 66, 68, 70–71
Jobs, Steve 101
Johnson, Spencer 54
Johnston, Sidney 4

Krantz, Judith 35
Kravis, Henry 69

Long, Huey 4

management: management literature 6, 54–56; popular management books 26–27, 31–34, 45; *see also* heroic manager
masculinity 65, 85, 107
McMahon, Linda 69
metaphor 28–30

metonymy 3–4, 11–12, 38–42, 91–92, 97
Mnuchin, Steve 69

Nader, Ralph 2–3
NBC 36
neoliberalism 5, 7, 16, 50–53, 56–57, 67, 76, 82, 91–92, 100, 107

Obama, Barack 79, 93–99
OPEC 59

Perelman, Ron 69
Perot, Ross 1, 71, 76, 78, 82–84, 89, 102
Peters, Tom 31, 34
populism 4, 15–16, 61, 67, 73, 83
prosopopoeia 16

Reagan, Ronald 5, 48, 51, 65–66, 78–79, 100
Reform Party 82–83, 89
Republican Party 57, 59, 95, 108
Romney, Mitt 2–4, 17, 85–87, 89–90, 97, 101–102
Roosevelt, Franklin Delano 78
Ross, Wilbur 69
Ryan, Tim 77, 79

Sandberg, Sheryl 77

Schlesinger, Arthur 91
Schwartz, Tony 24, 30
Sculley, John 46
Sinatra, Frank 108–109
Spielberg, Steven 35
Stallone, Sylvester 35–36, 109

Tillerson, Rex 69
Trump, Donald: *Art of the Deal* 9, 24–45, 76, 92, 95, 99, 108; *Art of the Comeback* 9, 30, 76; *Crippled America* 10, 98–100; *How to Get Rich* 76, 90; *Surviving at the Top* 9–10, 12, 30, 62–73, 76, 81, 89; *The America We Deserve* 10, 76, 89–90, 95; *The Apprentice* 10, 93–94, 98–99; *Time to Get Tough* 10, 94–100; and the Central Park Five 66, 71–72; and Twitter 2, 6, 10, 94, 108; and Republican Primary 2
The Trump Organization 11–12, 38–39, 97–98, 100
Turner, Ted 69

Waterman, Robert 31, 34
Welch, Jack 69
Winthrop, John 100
Wollman Rink 28–29, 38, 92
Wrapp, H. Edward 55

For Product Safety Concerns and Information please contact our EU representative GPSR@taylorandfrancis.com
Taylor & Francis Verlag GmbH, Kaufingerstraße 24, 80331 München, Germany

www.ingramcontent.com/pod-product-compliance
Lightning Source LLC
Chambersburg PA
CBHW070557170426
43201CB00012B/1869